ON THE PRIESTHOOD

ST. CHRYSOSTOM
TRANSLATED BY B. HARRIS COWPER

GLH Publishing
LOUISVILLE, KY

This translation published in 1866 by Williams and Norgate.

Public Domain

ISBN:
   Paperback 978-1-64863-122-1
   Epub 978-1-64863-123-8

For information on new releases, weekly deals, and free ebooks visit
www.GLHpublishing.com

Contents

Introduction 1

BOOK I.
I. Basil the best of all the friends of Chrysostom. 6
II. The unanimity of Basil and Chrysostom, and their common pursuits. 6
III. The balance becomes unequal on the question of adopting the monastic life. 6
IV. The proposal to have a common home. 7
V. His mother's lament. 7
VI. The fraud practised by Chrysostom in the matter of Basil's ordination. 8
VII. Basil's meek and gentle reproof. 9
VIII. Chrysostom's apology and recrimination. 11
IX. The great advantage of timely fraud. 13

BOOK II.
I. The Priesthood the greatest evidence of love to Christ. 16
II. The dignity of the Priesthood greater than that of other offices 17
III. The Priesthood requires a large and admirable spirit. 18
IV. The Priesthood full of extreme difficulty and danger. 19
V. Chrysostom avoided the office out of love to Christ. 22
VI. Proof of the virtue of Basil, and of his great love. 23
VII. Chrysostom did not avoid ordination because he intended to insult those who destined him for it. 24
VIII. Chrysostom even freed his friends from blame by his flight. 25

BOOK III.
I. They who suspected him of declining the Priesthood through arrogance, injured their own reputation. 27
II. He did not avoid it through vain glory. 28
III. If he had desired glory he would rather have chosen it. 28
IV. The Priesthood is something tremendous; and the priesthood of the New Testament is a much more solemn business than that of the old law. .. 28
V. The great authority and honour of priests. 29
VI. Priests the ministers of God's greatest gifts. 31
VII. S. Paul was awestruck when he contemplated the magnitude of this office. 32
VIII. He who enters upon this office is often led into sin unless he be a very noble-minded man. 33
IX. The man who is not of a noble spirit is ensnared by vain-glory, and its attendant evils. 33
X. The Priesthood not the cause of these evils, but our own dullness. 34
XI. The lust of domination is to be cast out of the soul of a Priest. 35
XII. A priest ought to be a very wise man. 36
XIII. Other requirements besides abstinence are looked for in a priest. 37
XIV. Mental purity and activity hindered by nothing so much as by inordinate anger. 37
XV. Another kind of conflict which is fraught with peril. 40
XVI. What sort of man he must be who has to encounter so many storms. .. 43
XVII. Great caution demanded by the spiritual oversight of virgins. 45

XVIII. The office of judge a difficult one. 47

BOOK IV.

I. Not only those who are anxious to enter the clerical office are severely corrected for the sins they commit, but those also who are constrained to accept it. 50
II. Such as ordain the unworthy will suffer the same punishment, even if they are unacquainted with those who are ordained. 54
III. Great ability to speak is required of a priest. 56
IV. The priest should be prepared to contend with Greeks (pagans), Jews, and heretics. 57
V. The priest ought to be well skilled in the art of reasoning. 58
VI. Evidence supplied by S. Paul. 59
VII. S. Paul was illustrious, not for his miracles only, but for his eloquence. ... 61
VIII. S. Paul would have us excel in a similar manner. 62
IX. If a priest is not endowed with such qualifications he must needs do much harm to his people 63

BOOK V.

I. Public discourses require much labour and study. 65
II. He that is appointed to the Priesthood ought to despise applause, and to be a powerful speaker. 65
III. He that has not both these endowments will be unprofitable to the people. 66
IV. Detraction should especially be treated with contempt. 66
V. The learned priest requires more diligence than the unlearned. 67
VI. The judgment of the unskilful multitude is not to be wholly despised, nor altogether regarded. 68
VII. What is said should be prepared only with the view of pleasing God. ... 69
VIII. He who is not supremely indifferent to praise will be subject to many troubles. 69

BOOK VI.

I. Priests are liable to correction for the sins of other men. 71
II. Priests require to be more circumspect than monks. 72
III. The monk is less embarrassed than the man who rules in the church. 72
IV. The priest is entrusted with authority over the world, and with other solemn duties. 73
V. The priest must be qualified for everything. 75
VI. To rule well in the Church is a greater proof of endurance than to be a monk. 76
VII. He who lives apart, and he who leads a public life have different cares. 76
VIII. It is more easy for such as dwell apart to practise virtue, than for such as have the care of many. 77
IX. Popular suspicion is not to be treated with contempt even when unfounded. 78
X. It is no great matter to save one oneself. 79
XI. A far severer punishment awaits the sins of priests than those of common men. 80
XII. Examples to show that sorrow and fear are caused by the anticipation of the priestly office. 81
XIII. Our conflict with the Devil is more grievous than any other. 84

INTRODUCTION

OF the translations of this work into other languages I need say nothing. Those which exist in English, so far as I can ascertain, are the following:—that of Hollier (London, 1728); that of Bunce (London, 1759); that of Hohler (Cambridge, 1837); and that of Marsh (London, 1844). All these may be regarded as books of uncommon occurrence. I have no occasion to speak of their merit. Only one of them has been before me during the execution of the present version. I refer to that by Mr. Hohler, which has undoubtedly many happy renderings, but not a few so ludicrously wrong that I have been amazed. Why, I know not, but I have been asked from time to time to do what I have now done. My first idea was to go carefully over one of the old versions and to republish it with any alterations which seemed necessary. But considering all the circumstances of the case, and that such a volume would at best be regarded as a mere *sartor resartus*, I resolved to translate the book for myself as soon as my leisure permitted. I have done so, and venture to lay the result before those who may be interested in it.

Although twenty years have come and gone since I made the acquaintance of the six books on the Priesthood, I send them forth with the same impressions as I received at the first: it is often difficult to convey the sense in tolerably intelligible English without a periphrasis; the work is one of extraordinary excellence, both for its language and its ideas; it will always be valuable to the aspirant to ministerial honour and usefulness; it is characterised by serious deficiencies which render other teachers necessary; and it is a remarkably interesting study for all who wish to know more of the Church of the latter half of the fourth century.

The opinions I have now uttered may be developed with some advantage.

1. With reference to the translation. I have said 'it is often difficult to convey the sense in tolerably intelligible English without a periphrasis;' and I may add that cases also occur in which I have felt it would be better for my readers if I slightly condensed the expression of the original. My aim has been throughout to steer as closely to the text as was possible without being excessively bald. Yet I have taken so much liberty in the construction of my sentences that I have not produced a mere *ordo verborum*. Consequently some may find that in construing the Greek, my version will not supersede the necessity for study. I wish it to be so. In rendering certain words I have not always used the same English term because it is notorious that many words must be viewed in their relations to the passages in which they stand. There are certain other words, chiefly technical and professional, with which I have desired to take no liberty whatever. If the terms of office employed by S. Chrysostom are really not always identical with those now in use in any branch of the Church, why should they be modernised to suit our practice? My aim herein has been to let my author speak for himself, in order that there may be no mistake

when words like 'priest,' 'presbyter,' 'minister,' 'bishop,' 'ruler,' and so forth occur. It may be urged that 'priest' and 'presbyter' are etymologically identical; and so they are in English, but practically they differ. Therefore when S. Chrysostom says, ἱερεύς, I put 'priest,' and where he has πρεσβύτερος, I have 'presbyter.' Again, there are certain metaphorical words which I found it simply impossible to reproduce in English, and these I have rendered *ad sensum* as I best could. The care I have taken to be faithful to my author is such that I hope few serious misrepresentations of his meaning will be found. There are places in which I have been compelled to differ from all previous translations, but in all such instances I have followed my deliberate judgment, and this is all I have to say about them. The text I have adopted is that of the well known Leipsic edition of Tauchnitz, because it is not only a good one, but the most widely circulated. A few of its deviations from the Benedictine edition have been indicated in the margin. Solely for the purpose of facilitating reference, I have retained the consecutive numeration of the short sections of the Leipsic book, and for the same cause have printed each as a distinct paragraph. The headings of the chapters are substantially the same as in the Greek, except in the third book where the Greek is deficient. The larger divisions of the Tauchnitz edition I have left unnoticed, because they do not always represent those which I have called chapters. For the division into chapters I have followed an edition of the Latin version of the Benedictines. With these explanations, I trust my principles and method will be understood: the execution must speak for itself.

2. I have said that the work of Chrysostom is 'one of extraordinary excellence both for its language and its ideas.' Its aim is to magnify the priestly office, and to render those who enter upon it conscious of their awful responsibilities. In his endeavours to realise this aim the author has wrought out a plot, which adds to the interest of the subject, and enables him to discuss the topics which may arise, in the form of a dialogue resting on a sort of narrative. Whether the events introduced actually occurred I know not, but in any case they are such as might have happened. Perhaps the solemn obligations imposed upon God's ministers were never more strikingly exhibited. Arguments, comparisons, texts of scripture, examples, and whatever may give force and energy to the main idea, are abundantly introduced. Those however, who would fully realise the lavish exuberance of resources must read the Greek, for no translation can accurately represent it. The composition of the book is such that I have been compelled to reject the old opinion that it was written in the early years of S. Chrysostom. The command of language, the solidity of judgment, and the profound knowledge of human nature and spiritual things here displayed, do not belong to the youthful and inexperienced.

3. I said the work 'will always be valuable to the aspirant to ministerial honour and usefulness.' He who aspires to the honour alone, will be likely to tremble under its terrible denunciations; but he who looks forward to usefulness in the Church of God may be led by it to earnest self-examination, to sincere humility, and to prayer for the grace of God to sustain and aid him in that for which no man alone is sufficient.

4. I said the book 'is characterised by serious deficiencies which render other

teachers necessary.' I suppose this will be admitted by all classes of readers, because the peculiarities of none of them are fully and exactly represented. This is true in relation to abstract doctrine, to forms and ceremonies, and to church discipline and government. Nothing is more natural than that we should persuade ourselves that the opinions and practices of our favourites agree with our own. Probably S. Chrysostom will be claimed by Roman and Anglican, by High Church and Evangelical, by Episcopalian and Congregationalist. So far as I can judge all will be right, and all will be wrong. The Romanist will find prayers for the dead, and the Anglican will observe no appeal to power external to the Church. The High Churchman will notice the exalted terms in which priestly dignity and sacramental efficacy are propounded; while the Evangelical will be gratified by the prominence given to God's grace and word and Spirit. The Episcopalian will see in Chrysostom a man who exalts the bishop's office with all his eloquence; and the Congregationalist will observe how at least the shadow of lay participation in ministerial appointments lingers on, how lay influence is recognised as perfectly legitimate when lawfully used, and how absolutely S. Chrysostom repudiates the civil power in matters of religion. Every party then, I have no doubt, may discover here what will seem to favour it. I am not aware that I am required to account for this circumstance, but I believe it my duty to mention it. Chrysostom may be none the worse Catholic for occupying such a position. But this very fact will justify the remark at the head of this paragraph. Those who claim our author because he has some of their characteristic features, will do their best to set him right where he does not come up to their standard. What he says which appears to be opposed to them, must be explained by means of an interpreter. His very silence on certain topics which are thought to be of importance in the respective sections of the Christian world must be accounted for. Why, for example, does he never mention the Virgin, the intercession of the saints, prayer to the saints, purgatory, the Bishop of Rome, etc.? Why is he silent as to all set forms of prayer, priestly vestments, incense, crosses, crossings, and a host of other matters? How is it that he does not clearly distinguish between the various orders of the clergy? Why is he so vague and indefinite in regard to some of the chief doctrines of Christianity? With reference to this last matter, it is true that he insists upon the necessity for a right faith, but many things are left unsaid, and there is a marked absence of much that would be acceptable to most. The Rev. C. Bridges notices this in his well-known work on 'The Christian Ministry,' where he says: "We must however, remark upon the evident deficiency of Chrysostom's treatise in those lively views and exercises of faith, which are the grand stimulants to our work.... His deficiency disables him indeed, as a sustaining comforter to the desponding minister." The elaborate vindication of deception when practised for a good end, will fail to satisfy many. The quotations from the Apocrypha will not please some. The entire argument in justification of the writer's own real or assumed evasion of the clerical office and work, will be regarded as adapted to keep back the timid as much as to repel the unworthy. Whatever position we occupy we shall find that this extraordinary production is not adequate as a representation of ministerial functions and encouragements. Its one grand feature is the manner in which it insists upon the awful responsibilities and obligations of the Christian priesthood. For our times, and for all times, it is of unspeakable value, but it is not enough alone, and recourse must be had to other teachers to make good its defects.

5. I said that the book 'is a remarkably interesting study for all who wish to know more of the Church of the latter half of the fourth century.' By this I mean that the book has an archæological value. It throws some light upon the condition of communities of monks, widows, and virgins. It suggests interesting reflections upon the choice and election of the clergy, and the position of the laity in regard to such occasions. It teaches us indirectly the relation of the Church to the secular and civil power, and a great many other matters which are more than curious. I cannot here indicate all the points which I have in view, but I imagine that a careful perusal of the work would help any one who desired to understand the inner life and action, and the external relations of the Church in the time of Chrysostom. Even what is said of the sacraments, of prayers for the dead, and of the state of the departed has an importance in the history of Christian doctrine.

I do not undertake to defend or to oppose any of the opinions advanced by S. Chrysostom in this work. It is true that he teaches baptismal regeneration, the power of priestly absolution, and at least the bodily presence of Christ in the Lord's Supper; that he views this last Sacrament as in some sense a sacrifice, and says the priest has to pray for the dead. It is true that he is silent as to tradition, and exalts the Scriptures as God's Word, and the source and standard of Christian truth. It is true that while he magnifies the priestly office and the importance of the prayers of the clergy, he makes the living word spoken or preached by them their great instrument, connecting with it the holiest of examples, and the most forcible reasoning. It is also true that he quotes the Apocryphal equally with the Canonical books; but never appeals to fathers, councils, or any other authorities. The sum and substance of all this perhaps is, that according to Chrysostom the Holy Scriptures are God's supreme and sole law in the Church, and the clergy are entrusted with power to interpret, preach, defend, and enforce that law in the name of God for the Church's good. It follows, that while God rules the clergy by the Scriptures, the clergy rule the Church mainly by the same means. This is my understanding of our author's general principle, and I leave others to see whether I am correct or not.

I have overlooked one matter which may require a word of explanation: I find that some previous translators have frequently introduced the word 'Bishop' where the Greek has it not, and have from time to time translated ἱερεύς by 'Bishop.' This has perhaps been done to produce apparent consistency. But I have not followed the example set me, for two reasons: first, because such a proceeding seemed opposed to my principle of never making S. Chrysostom say what he did not certainly mean; secondly, because the book is distinctly intitled, 'Of the Priesthood,' and therefore should not be taken as primarily a manual for bishops, but for such as had not received full clerical orders. If I am not wrong the term 'Priesthood' here fairly includes 'Bishops, Priests, and Deacons.'

The conditions which I have imposed upon myself have not allowed me to attempt the production of a graceful and eloquent composition. I have tried to catch the spirit of the original, and have not been inattentive to its form. But it is confessedly beyond my command of language, if it be not more than the English tongue is equal to, to imitate the precision and elegance of the Greek. If it should be thought that my phraseology falls far short of the original, and is from time to time even colloquial, I could not deny it. S. Chrysostom himself manifestly endeavours often to speak familiarly and freely, but then he also often soars away in a style which is inimitable. Even at his best however, I should be sorry to compare him with the great and grand masters of Grecian oratory. The power and beauty which this noble language exhibits in his hands, is, after all, a power and beauty which has passed its meridian. We admire the intellect, piety, earnestness, and eloquence of the speaker, but we are conscious that his language is shorn of its glory.

The reader will observe that I have not undertaken the labour of annotating the translation. But I have endeavoured to point out in the margin many passages of Scripture which are directly or indirectly referred to in the text.

B. H. C.
LONDON,
February, 1866.

Book I.

I. Basil the best of all the friends of Chrysostom.

1. I HAD many friends, both genuine and true, who understood and strictly observed the laws of friendship; but among the many there was one who far excelled them all in attachment to me, and strove to leave the rest as far behind, as they did such as were simply well disposed towards me.

2. He was one of those who always accompanied me, for we had embraced the same studies, and availed ourselves of the same instructors; we had the same inclination and zeal for the subjects which occupied us; while our aspirations were alike, and produced by the same influences. Nor was this only while we waited upon our preceptors, but also when, on leaving them, we had to advise what was the best course of life for us to choose. And even here it appeared we were of one accord.

II. The unanimity of Basil and Chrysostom, and their common pursuits.

3. And other things, in addition to these, preserved our unanimity firm and unbroken. For the one could not boast more than the other about the greatness of his country; nor had I superfluous wealth, while he subsisted in extreme penury. Moreover, the similarity of our aim corresponded with the moderateness of our means. Our condition in life also was of the same degree, and everything concurred with our disposition.

III. The balance becomes unequal on the question of adopting the monastic life.

4. But when the time was come for my dear friend to adopt the monastic life, and the true philosophy, this our balance was no longer equal, inasmuch as his scale became light and went up, while I, still fettered by the desires of the world, drew mine down, and was forced to stay below, burdening it with youthful fancies.

5. Here, for the rest, our friendship continued firm as before; but our intercourse was interrupted, because it was impossible for such as were not zealous in the same pursuits, to have a common rendezvous.

6. But when I myself lifted up my head a little above the storm of life, he seized me with both his hands. Even thus, however, we were unable to preserve our former equality; for, having got the start of me in point of time, and having displayed great alacrity, he was again carried above me, and borne to a great elevation.

IV. THE PROPOSAL TO HAVE A COMMON HOME.

7. Nevertheless, being a good man, and valuing my friendship highly, he separated himself from all others, and continued always with me. Of this he had been desirous before, but, as I said, he was prevented by my remissness.

8. For it could not be that one who frequented the court of justice, and followed the pleasures of the stage, should be very often in the company of one who was attached to his books, and never came into public.

9. Therefore, though prevented before, yet when he welcomed me into the same manner of life as his own, he speedily brought forth the desire he had long travailed with, and did not endure to leave me even the smallest part of the day, and went on entreating that each should leave his own home, and that we should have a common residence. Well, he persuaded me, and the event was at hand.

V. HIS MOTHER'S LAMENT.

10. But the continual appeals of my mother prevented me from granting him this favour, or rather, from receiving this gift from him. For when she perceived that I designed this, she took me by the hand, and led me into the apartment assigned to her; and having seated me near the couch whereon she had travailed with me, she shed fountains of tears, and added words more piteous than tears, lamenting to me in this wise:—

11. "I, my child," said she, "was not long permitted to enjoy the virtue of your father, for so it pleased God, since his death which succeeded the pains I bore for you, brought orphanhood upon you, and untimely widowhood upon me, and the horrors of widowhood, which only they who suffer can rightly understand.

12. No language could describe the storm and tempest which a damsel endures, who has but just come from her father's house, and is practically inexperienced,—when she is suddenly smitten with unbearable grief, and compelled to undertake anxieties too great for her age and sex.

13. She must, I suppose, encounter the slothfulness of domestics, and keep an eye upon their misdeeds, ward off the plots of relatives, and bravely bear the insults of those who levy the public taxes, and their cruelty in the imposition of tribute.

14. And, moreover, if the dead should leave a child when he departs, and it happens to be a girl, even this will cause the mother much anxiety; severed, although it is, from expense and fear. But a son fills her every day with ten thousand fears, and still more anxieties, for I leave out the outlay of money which she is forced to submit to, if she desires to bring him up respectably.

15. Still, none of these things persuaded me to contract a second marriage, and to bring another bridegroom into your father's house; but I persisted in my tumult and trouble, and did not retreat from the iron furnace of widowhood, for I was specially supported by an influence from above.

16. And it brought me no slight comfort in these sad trials, to look continually in your face, and to observe the living image of him that was dead, and one fashioned so much like him. On this account, while you were yet a child, and had not even learned to talk, when especially children delight their parents, you yielded me

great comfort.

17. Neither was it in your power to say and complain, that I endured my widowhood nobly, and yet diminished your paternal estate through the requirements of that widowhood, as I know has happened to many, who have unfortunately become orphans; for I have preserved all this untouched. Yet I have omitted nothing that ought to have been expended to your advantage, but have paid for it out of my own property, and with what I had when I left my home.

18. Do not suppose that in saying this I am finding fault; but in return for all these things I ask one favour of you,—not to involve me in a second widowhood, nor to kindle again the grief which now smoulders, but to wait for my decease. Perhaps after a short time I shall depart.

19. For there is a hope that the young may come to distant old age; but we who are old, await nothing but death.

20. When, therefore, you have committed me to the earth, and have mingled my bones with your father's, undertake long journeys, and sail over what seas you choose. Then there will be no one to hinder you. But while I have breath, bear to reside with me. Do not offend God idly and for nought, by involving in so great ills me who have done you no wrong.

21. If, indeed, you have to complain that I entangle you in worldly cares, and compel you to manage my concerns, do not respect the laws of nature, nor your rearing, nor intimacy, nor anything else, but flee from me as a traitress and a foe. But if I do all I can to provide much leisure for you in your journey through this life, even though nothing else should, let this bond retain you with me.

22. For if you say that thousands love you, not one will enable you to enjoy so much liberty; because there is no one whose concern for your advantage will equal mine."

VI. THE FRAUD PRACTISED BY CHRYSOSTOM IN THE MATTER OF BASIL'S ORDINATION.

23. This, and more than this, my mother said to me, and I told it to my magnanimous friend; who was not only not disheartened by the words, but urged me even more, making the same request as formerly.

24. While matters remained in this position, he constantly entreating, and I not consenting, a rumour which suddenly sprang up, agitated both of us. Now the rumour was, that we were about to be advanced to the priestly dignity.

25. As for myself, on hearing this report, I was seized with fear and perplexity: with fear, lest I should be taken against my will; and with perplexity, asking repeatedly whence it had come to those men that any such thing should be desired of me, for on considering myself, I found that I had nothing to make me worthy of that honour.

26. But my noble-minded friend, coming to me privately, and communing with me about the matter, as if I had not heard the rumour, entreated, that in this case as before, it might be seen we were alike in deed and counsel; because he would readily follow me, in whichever course I took the lead, whether we had to avoid or to accept.

27. Perceiving his willingness, and thinking I should bring loss on the whole community of the Church, if, through my weakness, I deprived the flock of Christ of a young man so good, and so adapted to preside over men, I did not reveal to him my intention in the matter, although I had never before allowed him to be unaware of any of my purposes; but saying that the consideration of these things must be postponed to another time (for it was not now urgent), I persuaded him forthwith not to trouble himself upon the subject, and in regard to myself, I gave him encouragement, as though I should be of one mind with him, if such an event ever took place.

28. But after a short time had elapsed, and he who was going to ordain us had come, and I had hidden myself, he (Basil) who knew nothing of it, was led away as though for another purpose, and received the yoke, hoping, after the promise I had made him, that I should at all events follow him, or rather, thinking he was following me.

29. Moreover, some of those who were present there, seeing that he was vexed at being caught, deceived him by exclaiming, how strange it was that he who seemed in all things to be the bolder (meaning me), should yield with so much meekness to the judgment of the fathers; and that he who was the more prudent and gentle, should be so bold and vain in restiveness, drawing back and gainsaying.

30. After yielding to these remonstrances, when he heard that I had retreated, he came to me in great dejection, and sat down by me, and intended to say something, but was prevented by his perplexity, and could not find the power he needed to speak: when he opened his mouth utterance was choked, for his mental distress interrupted his speech before it passed his lips.

31. Therefore, seeing him all in tears, and full of his great trouble, and knowing the cause, I smiled for extreme pleasure, and taking him by the hand, I strove to kiss it, and praised God, that the result of my stratagem was favourable, and such as I had always desired.

32. But when he saw me joyous and cheerful, and discovered that he had been deceived by me before, he was even more vexed and annoyed.

VII. Basil's meek and gentle reproof.

And when he had somewhat suppressed the tumult of his soul, he said:—

[BASIL.] If you have renounced my interests, and have no further respect and consideration for me, (why so, I know not,) you should still be careful of your own reputation. But now you have opened all men's mouths, and all say you have refused this ministry through love of vain glory; and there is no one who can deliver you from such an accusation.

33. I cannot even bear to appear in public, so many come to me and revile me daily; for when they see me anywhere in the city, those who are at all intimate with me, take me aside and subject me to the chief share of the blame. For, say they, you who knew his mind (and none of his interests was hidden from you), should not have kept it to yourself, but ought to have imparted it to us, and we should not have been by any means unprovided with a scheme for his capture.

34. Now inasmuch as I did not know you had long since resolved upon this, I

am put to shame, and I blush to tell them, lest they should suppose our friendship to be mere pretence. But if it is so, and verily it is, and you cannot deny it, after what you have now done in regard to me, it would still be well to conceal our failings from those who are without, and yet entertain a moderately good opinion of us.

35. I am reluctant to tell them the truth, and how the case stands between us, and so I am compelled to keep silence, and to bend towards the ground, and to avoid those who are coming towards me, and to get out of the way.

36. For even if I escaped the former censure, I must afterwards of necessity be condemned for mendacity. Because they will never believe that you range Basil alongside of others who are not suffered to know your affairs.

37. But I have not much to say about these things, inasmuch as it has thus seemed good to you: and how shall we bear the shame of what yet remains? Some accuse you of caprice, and some, of vain glory; while the more unsparing of those that complain charge us with both together, and add that we have insulted those who have honoured us.

38. They say they should have suffered justly, even if they had been yet more dishonoured by us, because they passed by so many and so worthy men, and hastily invested with such honour as they never even dreamed to expect to receive, two striplings who but a day or two ago were still entangled by the cares of life, and who but a very short time had worn a sober countenance, and put on grave garments, and affected seriousness. Moreover, those who from early life to advanced age have performed their discipline, are among those who are under authority, and boys who have not even learned the laws by which rule should be exercised, direct them. Men who say these things and more than these, constantly assail me.

39. Now I am at a loss what answer I shall make to these things; so I pray you, tell me. For I do not think you took to flight heedlessly and without cause, and incurred the enmity of men who are so great, but that you were led to it with some reasoning and consideration, wherefore I also conjecture you have some reply ready by way of defence. Say then whether we can offer any just pretext to those who accuse us?

40. For I ask no apology for what I have been wronged in by you, nor for the deception you have practised, nor for your betrayal of me, nor for the advantages you have received through me at any former time.

41. For, if I may so say, I brought and placed my very soul in your hands; but you have used as much guile with me, as if you had needed to be on your guard against an enemy.

42. Yet you ought not to have avoided the gain yourself if you supposed this project beneficial; but if injurious, you ought to have delivered from harm myself also, whom you have always professed to honour above all others.

43. But you have done all you could to make me fall into the snare, and must needs have recourse to guile and hypocrisy, against one who had ever been wont to speak and act with you in everything honestly and frankly.

44. Nevertheless, in what I have said, I accuse you of none of these things now, nor do I reproach you on account of the loneliness in which you have placed me, by interrupting those conferences from which we often derived no ordinary pleasure and profit.

45. But I dismiss all these things, and endure them in silence and with meekness; not because you have slightly transgressed against me, but because I laid down for myself this law from the very day when I began to cherish affection for you,—that however willing you might be to grieve me, I would never impose upon you the necessity of an apology.

46. For that you have brought upon me no little injury, you yourself also know, if you but remember the words which have always been spoken of us by others as well as by ourselves. They were to this effect:—that it was a great gain for us to be of one accord, and that we were fortified by our affection towards each other.

47. And all said that our unanimity would confer no little benefit upon many besides. Yet I never imagined, so far as I am concerned, that I should render services to any; but I said we should realise from it at least this return, that those who sought to enter into conflict with us would find us hard to overcome.

48. Nor did I ever cease to remind you of this: "The time is one of difficulty; those who take counsel against us are many; the genuineness of love is perished, and the pest of detraction has been put in its place; we travel in the midst of snares, and walk about on the battlements of cities; those who are ready to exult in our misfortunes if anything should happen, are many and have beset us on every side; there is no one to condole with us, or at any rate such are very few; beware lest by separating we should at any time provoke great ridicule, and mischief surpassing the ridicule. Brother helped by brother is like a strong city, and a well fortified kingdom; do not dissolve this relationship, nor break down this barrier."

49. This and more than this I was always saying, never suspecting anything of this sort, but supposing you were perfectly sound in regard to me, I only superfluously wished to heal one that was well. But it seems I was unwittingly administering remedies to a sick man. I was unfortunate enough to do no good, and no advantage has accrued to me from my excessive forethought.

50. For, casting all these things away, and not even giving them a thought, you abandoned me like a ship without ballast in an untried ocean, without considering those wild waves which I must encounter.

51. For if ever calumny, or ridicule, or any other reproach or insult should happen to be heaped upon me,—and such things often necessarily occur,—to whom shall I flee? To whom impart my grief? Who will be ready to protect me, and will restrain those who vex me, and cause them to vex me no more? Who will comfort me, and fit me to bear with the follies of others? There is no one; because you stand afar off from this dreadful conflict, and cannot so much as hear the clamour.

52. Know you not what mischief you have done? And even now, after you have smitten, do you perceive how deadly is the wound you have inflicted on me?

53. But put aside these matters,—for you cannot undo what has been done, nor find an explanation for the inexplicable,—what shall we say to others? What answer can we give to their accusations?

VIII. CHRYSOSTOM'S APOLOGY AND RECRIMINATION.

[CHRYSOSTOM.] 54. Take heart, said I; for I am not only ready to rectify all this, but I will attempt, to the best of my ability, to render you an account for the very matters wherein you freed me from responsibility; and, if you will, the beginning and first words of my defence shall be from them.

55. For I should be very stupid and irrational, if, while caring for the opinions of others, and doing all I can to make them cease from calumniating me, I should be unable to persuade the man who is dearest of all to me, (and pays me so much respect as not to accuse me even of what he says I have wronged him in, but accounting his own interests nothing, still is anxious for mine), that I do not wrong him, but should seem to manifest towards him an indifference which is greater than the zeal he has shown for me.

56. Wherein then have I wronged you? For hence have I determined to embark on the sea of my defence: is it that I have circumvented you, and concealed my intention? Still it was for the profit of you who were deceived, and of those to whom I delivered you when I had deceived you.

57. If indeed all guile be evil, and one is never to employ it when expedient, I am prepared to pay what penalty you will; or rather, since you will never bear to inflict punishment upon me, I shall pronounce on myself the same sentence as judges pronounce upon criminals when the plaintiffs carry conviction.

58. But if an act be not always wrong, but becomes bad or good according to the motive of the doer, cease to accuse me for deceiving, and show that I devised it for evil; for so long as this is not done, it would only be just that such as desire to be well-disposed, should not bring rebukes and accusations upon him that has practised deceit, but should even express their approval of him.

59. For deceit when well-timed and practised with a right intention, is so profitable that many have often been punished because they have not circum vented.

60. And if you will search into the records of the most celebrated military commanders since the world began, you will find that most of their trophies were the results of stratagem, and that these have been applauded rather than those who have conquered in the open field.

61. For these carry on their wars with a much greater expenditure both of money and of men, so that they gain nothing beyond their victory, but the conquerors are no less injured than the defeated, in the sacrifice of armies as well as in the emptying of treasuries; and besides, men do not allow them to enjoy all the glory consequent on victory, for it comes to pass that no small share of it is the portion of those who have fallen, seeing that conquering in spirit they were defeated in body alone: therefore, if the willing had been fated not to fall, and death had not come in to stop them, they would never have cast aside their bravery.

62. But he that is able to conquer by stratagem involves his enemies not only in misfortune but ridicule. For it is not here in reference to prudence, as it is in the other case on the score of valour, where both carry off equal praises, but the whole of the prize falls to the victors; and, what is no less, they preserve for the state, unsullied, the pleasure of victory. Prudence of mind is not like abundance of resources, and a multitude of men; for whereas these are apt to be expended and to fail those who have them, when one constantly employs them in wars,—this, the more it is called into action, the more it is increased.

63. We may find the use of deceit to be great and needful, not only in war, but also in peace; and not in affairs of state only, but also at home,—by the husband

towards the wife, and by the wife towards her husband, and by the father towards the son, and by friend towards friend, and even by children towards a father.

64. For the daughter of Saul could not otherwise deliver her husband out of the hands of Saul, than by defrauding her father;[1] and her brother, who wished to save him whom she had delivered, when he was again in danger, used the same weapons as the woman had done.[2]

IX. THE GREAT ADVANTAGE OF TIMELY FRAUD.

[BASIL.] 65. And Basil said: None of these things apply to me, because I am not a foe and an enemy, nor one of those who attempt to injure, but altogether the opposite; for I have always committed all my affairs to your judgment, and have followed what you enjoined.

[CHRYSOSTOM.] 66. But, my admirable and most excellent friend, for this very cause I have already said it was well to employ it (deceit), not only in war and against our foes, but also in peace and towards those who are most dear to us.

67. For that it is beneficial not only to the deceivers, but to the deceived, go and ask any of the physicians, how they deliver from disease such as are sick, and you will learn from them that they are not content with their skill alone, but sometimes by availing themselves of deceit, and combining with their art the help it renders, they have in this way restored the sick to health.

68. For when the peevishness of the patient, and the obstinacy of the complaint refuse to submit to the advice of the physicians, then it is necessary to assume the mask of deceit, in order that, as on the stage, they may be able to conceal the truth of the case.

69. But, if you please, I will narrate to you a case of fraud, one among many which I have heard of the sons of the physicians practising.[3] A fever once attacked a person suddenly and with great violence, and his burning heat was intense; but the patient refused what could have quenched the fire, while he longed and greatly urged, beseeching all who approached him, that they would give him plenty of undiluted wine, and enable him to satiate his ruinous craving. If any one had granted him this favour, not merely would he have aggravated the fever, he would have thrown the unhappy man into delirium.

70. Skill was here of no avail, and had no resources, but was wholly set aside; whereas deceit came in and showed its power to be so great as you will speedily hear from me.

71. For the physician, coming with an earthenware cup fresh from the furnace, and dipping it into a quantity of wine, afterwards emptied it; then, having filled it with water, he gave orders for the chamber where the patient lay to be darkened with a number of curtains, so that the light should not expose the fraud; after which he offered it him to drink as if it had been full of undiluted wine.

1 1 Sam. xix. 12.

2 1 Sam. xx. 11.

3 'Sons of the physicians' is, of course, equivalent to the 'medical tribe,' 'medical profession,' or simply 'physicians,' but it seemed best to retain the idiom.

72. But being at once, and before he took it into his hands, deceived by the odour which it emitted, he could not stop to pry narrowly into what was given him, but trusting to this (the smell), deceived by the darkness, and urged by his longing, he very eagerly drank off what was offered him; and having been sated by it, he shook off the choking sensation at once, and escaped from imminent peril.

73. Do you see the benefit of deceit? and if one would enumerate all the frauds of physicians his discourse would run to an unlimited length.

74. We may say, that this remedy has been continually employed, not only by those who heal the body, but by those who have the care of spiritual diseases. In this way the blessed Paul attracted those many myriads of Jews;[4] with this intention he circumcised Timothy,[5] who yet admonished the Galatians that Christ will profit nothing such as are circumcised;[6] and for this cause he became subject to the law, who accounted the righteousness which is by the law, a loss when one has faith in Christ.[7]

75. Great is the power of deceit, provided it be not had recourse to with a crafty intention: or rather, such ought not to be called deceit, but a sort of good management, and wisdom, and skill which can invent many resources where resources fail, and can correct the errors of the mind.

76. I should not say that Phinehas was a murderer, although he killed two persons at one blow;[8] nor should I call Elijah one, because of the hundred soldiers and their captains,[9] and the great torrent of blood which flowed when he caused the slaughter of those who were the priests of demons.[10]

77. For if we assented to this, and any one tested actions by themselves, excluding the intention of the doers, he who liked might condemn even Abraham for child-murder,[11] and accuse his grandson and his descendant of malice and fraud; for in this way one acquired the birthright, and the other conveyed the riches of the Egyptians to the host of the Israelites.[12]

78. But it is certainly not so: away with such audacity! for we do not merely acquit them of blame, we even admire them for these things, because God also has praised them for them.

79. He indeed would justly be called a deceiver, who employed the device

---

4 Acts xxi. 26.

5 Acts xvi. 3.

6 Gal. v. 2.

7 Phil. iii. 6-9.

8 Numb. xxv. 7, 8.

9 2 Kings i. 9-12.

10 1 Kings xviii. 40.

11 Gen. xxii. 1-14.

12 Gen. xxvii. 1-40; Exod. ii. 2, 3.

unjustly, [not he who does so with a wholesome intention],[13] and one must often deceive and confer the greatest benefit by that expedient; but he that has been prompted to act in a straightforward manner, has often done great mischief to the man whom he has not deceived.

---

13 These words in brackets do not appear in the Leipaic edition.

Book II.

I. The Priesthood the Greatest Evidence of Love to Christ.

80. It could be shown even yet more fully that it is possible to employ the influence of deceit for good, or rather, that in such a case we ought not to call it deceit, but a sort of management worthy of our admiration. But since what I have said is sufficient demonstration, it would be burdensome and tedious to carry my discourse to an unnecessary length; and it remains for you to prove that I have not used this very thing to your advantage.

[Basil.] 81. Then said Basil: And what advantage has occurred to me from this management, or wisdom, or whatever you may please to call it; that I may be convinced I have not been deceived by you?

[Chrysostom.] 82. What can exceed this advantage, said I,—that you have been seen to perform what Christ himself declared to be the evidences of love to Christ?

83. For addressing the chief of the Apostles, He said, "Peter, lovest thou me?" And when he confessed that he did, He added, "If thou lovest me, feed my sheep."[14]

84. The Master asked the disciple if he loved Him, not that He might obtain information, for how should He do this, who searches the hearts of all men? but that He might teach us how much He is concerned in the superintendence of these sheep. And since this is manifest, it will also be evident, that a great and unspeakable recompense will await him who labours in those things which Christ esteems so much.

85. For if, when we see any concerned for our domestics, and families, and flocks, we regard their zeal for them as a sign of love to us,—although all this can be bought for money,—with how great a recompense will He, who not with money nor any such thing, but by his own death purchased this flock, and gave his own blood as the price of this herd, reward those who tend it?

86. When therefore the disciple said, "Thou knowest, Lord, that I love thee," and appealed to the Beloved One Himself as the witness of his love, the Saviour did not stop at this, but added that which was the token of love.

87. He did not wish to show then how much Peter loved him, because this already appeared in many ways, but how much He himself loved his own Church, and He wished Peter and all of us to learn that we also should display great zeal for the same objects.

88. Why did God not spare his only-begotten Son, but gave him up, although his only one?[15] It was that He might reconcile those who had been his enemies, and

---

14 John xxi. 15.

15 Rom. viii. 32.

make them a peculiar people.[16] Why did He shed his blood? It was that He might purchase those sheep which He committed to Peter and to those who come after him.

89. Christ therefore said rightly, "Who then is that faithful and wise servant, whom his lord has appointed over his household."[17] The words again are those of one who doubts, though the speaker uttered them without doubting; but, as when He asked Peter if he loved Him, He inquired although he did not need to learn the disciple's affection, but wished to show the vast extent of his own love: So too now, when He says, "Who is a faithful and wise servant?" He says it not because He knows not who is faithful and wise, but because He wills to show the rarity of such endowments, and the greatness of this office. Notice how great is the reward: "He shall appoint him ruler over all his goods."[18]

II. THE DIGNITY OF THE PRIESTHOOD GREATER THAN THAT OF OTHER OFFICES.

90. Will you then still dispute with me about not being rightly deceived, when you are going to be set over all that is God's, and to do that which when Peter did, (the Lord) said he should he enabled to excel the rest of the Apostles? For he said, "Peter, lovest thou me more than these?"[19]

91. And although He could have said to him, 'If thou lovest me, practise fasting, sleeping on the ground, and constant vigils; look after those who are injured; be a father to the fatherless, and instead of a husband to their mother;' yet, setting aside all these things, what does He say? "Feed my sheep."

92. For many, even of such as are under authority, and not merely men but women, would be able easily to perform what is afore-mentioned; but when it is needful to preside over churches, and to be entrusted with the care of so many souls, let the entire womanly sex give way before the magnitude of the task, and the majority of men as well.

93. Let those be introduced to the arena, who far excel all others, and are as much above others in eminence of spirit, as Saul was above the whole Hebrew nation in bodily stature.[20]

94. For here, let me not merely require elevated shoulders; but let the distance between the pastor and his charge be as great as the difference between rational men and irrational creatures, that I say not even greater; because the danger affects much greater interests.

95. He who loved his sheep, would perhaps obtain forgiveness from the owner of the flock, whether wolves seized them, or robbers made a raid upon them, or

---

16 Tit. ii. 14.

17 Matth. xxiv. 45.

18 Matth. xxiv. 47.

19 John xxi. 15. Here some add the words, "feed my sheep."

20 1 Sam. x. 23.

any pestilence or other calamity befell them; and even if he suffered punishment, his loss would extend only to property. But he that has had confided to him the rational flock of Christ is first of all subject to loss, not of money, but of his own soul, through the perishing of the sheep.

96. And then, he has a far greater and more difficult conflict; for his contest is not with wolves, and he has no fear of robbers, nor is his concern to drive away a pestilence from the flock.

97. But against whom is his war? With whom is his battle? Hear the blessed Paul, who says, "For we wrestle, not against flesh and blood, but against principalities, against powers, against the world-rulers of the darkness of this world, and against spiritual evils, in heavenly places."[21] Do you see the terrible host of enemies, and the fierce phalanxes, not armed with swords, but naturally supplied with the substitute for a whole panoply?

98. Would you also see another army, stern and cruel, which lies in wait for this flock? You will see this too from the same watch-tower. For he who has spoken about the others, also indicates these enemies to us, speaking in this wise: "Now the works of the flesh are manifest, which are fornication, adultery, uncleanness, lasciviousness, idolatry, poisoning, enmities, contentions, jealousies, altercations, slanderings, whisperings, arrogance, and seditions;"[22] and others besides these, for he did not enumerate them all, but left us to understand the rest from these.

99. In regard to the pastor of irrational creatures, when those who wish to destroy the flock, see him that is over it fleeing away, they cease from contention with him, and are satisfied with the plunder of the cattle. But here, even if they capture all the flock, they do not then refrain from the shepherd, but the rather endeavour, and dare the more, and cease not until they either smite him down or are themselves overcome.

100. And in addition to this, the afflictions of cattle are apparent, whether famine, or pestilence, or wounds, or anything else which distresses them; and this would assist not a little in the relief of such as are troubled.

101. And there is also something else which more than this facilitates deliverance from such affliction. And what is that? Shepherds, with great authority compel the sheep to receive the remedy when they do not willingly submit; for it is easy to bind them when incision or cautery is necessary, and to keep them in for a long time when this is beneficial, and to give them one kind of food instead of another, and to restrain them from their supplies of water; and they very easily bring to bear anything else which they may think conducive to their health.

III. THE PRIESTHOOD REQUIRES A LARGE AND ADMIRABLE SPIRIT.

102. But, in the first place, it is not easy for a man to detect the infirmities of men; for "no man knoweth the things of a man, but the spirit of a man which is in him."[23] How then is any one to apply the remedy for a disease of which he knows not the

---

21 Eph. vi. 12.

22 Gal. v. 19, 20.

23 1 Cor. ii. 11.

symptoms, and is often unable to understand whether a man is really sick?

103. And even when this becomes apparent, it causes him yet more difficulty; for all men cannot be prescribed for with as much authority as a shepherd doctors his sheep. Now in this case also, there is need of binding, and restraining from food, and of cautery, and incision; but the power to administer the medicine, is not with him who supplies the remedy, but rather with the patient. That wonderful man (St. Paul) recognising this also, said to the Corinthians: "Not that we have dominion over your faith, but we are helpers of your joy."[24]

104. It is permitted to Christians less than any, to correct by force the faults of those who sin. But secular judges, when they bring malefactors under the laws, show their authority to be great, and prevent them, even against their will, from following their own courses. Here, however, we must make such a man better, not by compulsion but by persuasion.

105. Because we have not received from the laws such great authority to restrain them that sin; even if they gave it us, we should not have opportunity to use the power, because God crowns, not such as abstain from evil through necessity, but by choice.

106. Therefore, much art is needed that the sick may willingly persuade themselves to submit to the remedies provided by the priests; and not only so, but that they may be thankful to them for the cure.

107. If any one that is bound should be restive (for he is master of himself in this), he would make the mischief worse; and if he should reject the words which cut like a knife, he would inflict a new wound by his contempt, and the intention to heal becomes the occasion of a worse disease; because no one, by using compulsion, can cure an unwilling man.

IV. THE PRIESTHOOD FULL OF EXTREME DIFFICULTY AND DANGER.

108. What then is to be done? For if you deal too gently with him that requires a large incision, and do not inflict a deep wound upon him that has need of it, you remove one part of the sore, and the other part you leave.

109. But if you make the incision you ought without sparing, the patient is often driven to desperation by his pains, hastily casts everything aside, both application and bandages, and throws himself headlong, breaking his bond and tearing asunder the ligature. I could tell of many who have rushed into the most extreme evils because the due penalty for their sins was exacted.

110. For we ought not to inflict a punishment which accords with the measure of transgressions, but inquiry must be made as to the disposition of those who sin; lest while you desire to mend what is torn you make the rent worse, and while you endeavour to restore what is fallen you make the ruin greater.

111. For those who are infirm and remiss, and for the most part entangled in the pleasures of the world, and those who, on account of their family and influence, may be high spirited, should be turned away from the things wherein they sin, gently and little by little, and be delivered, if not altogether, at least in part from the evils which controul them. But if one should apply speedy discipline, he would

---

24 2 Cor. i. 24.

deprive them of the least amendment.

112. For when the soul is once compelled to abandon its sense of shame, it lapses into insensibility, and afterwards neither yields to kind words, nor succumbs to admonitions, nor is influenced by favours, but becomes far worse than the city which the prophet rebuked, saying: "Thou hast the face of a harlot, thou hast behaved without shame towards all men."[25]

113. Therefore the pastor has need of great understanding and of a myriad eyes, in order to observe on every side the habitudes of the soul.

114. For, as many are lifted up into presumption and fall into despondency about their own salvation, through being unable to bear bitter remedies; so there are some who, because they do not suffer a punishment equivalent to their sins, slide into negligence, become far worse, and are led on to sin yet more.

115. Therefore none of these things must be unattended to, but he that has been made a priest, when he has minutely investigated everything, should appositely employ what he has, that the zeal he possesses may not be in vain.

116. And one may see that he has many things to do, not in this alone, but in combining the severed members of the Church.

117. For the shepherd of the sheep has the flock following him whithersoever he leads; and if any of them should turn aside out of the right way, and leaving the good pasture, should feed in barren and precipitous places, it suffices for him to call aloud to bring them back again, and to restore to the fold that which had gone astray.

118. But if a man should wander from the right faith, the shepherd will require much exertion, endurance and patience; for he is not to be dragged back by force, nor to be compelled by fear, but you must restore him by persuasion, to the truth from which at first he fell.

119. He must therefore be of a noble spirit; that he may not be overcome by his difficulties, and despair of the salvation of the wanderers, and that he may constantly reason and say thus with himself: "Perhaps God may grant them the acknowledgment of the truth, and deliver them out of the snare of the devil."[26]

120. Therefore, the Lord, when conversing with his disciples, said: "Who then is the faithful and prudent servant?"[27] For he who exercises himself confers advantage on himself alone; but the profit of the pastoral function pervades a whole people. He who distributes his goods among the poor, or in other ways succours the distressed, has to some extent benefited his neighbours, but as much less than the priest does, as the distance is between the body and the soul.

121. Rightly, therefore, did the Lord say, that care for His sheep was a sign of love to Him.

[BASIL.] 122. And you, said he, do you not love Christ?

---

25 Jer iii. 3.

26 2 Tim. ii. 25. Another reading is: "If peradventure God should give them repentance unto the acknowledgment of the truth, and that they may be recovered out of the snare of the devil."

27 Matt. xxiv. 45.

[CHRYSOSTOM.] I both love, and will never cease to love Him; but I feared lest I should offend Him that is loved by me.

[BASIL.] 123. And what enigma, said he, could be more unintelligible than this?—if indeed Christ has commanded him that loves Him to feed His sheep, and you mean that therefore you do not feed them, because you love Him that commanded this!

[CHRYSOSTOM.] 124. What I say is no enigma, said I, but very intelligible and simple. For if I were able to administer this authority as Christ willed, and then forsook it, I ought to be in doubt as to what I say; but inasmuch as weakness of mind renders me useless for this ministry, wherein does what I have said call for discussion?

125. I am afraid too, lest, by undertaking to manage the flock of Christ when it is healthy and well fed, and then ruining it by my unskilfulness, I should provoke against myself, God, who so loved it as to give up Himself for its salvation and ransom.

[BASIL.] 126. You say these things in sport, said he; for if you are in earnest I know not how you would prove that I am justly grieved, otherwise than by the very words whereby you have endeavoured to drive away my perplexity. I knew even before that you had deceived and betrayed me; but much more now when you have undertaken to get rid of my accusations, do I learn and clearly understand what evils you have led me into.

127. For if you withdrew from such a ministry, for this reason, that you were conscious your mind was unequal to the burden of the task, I ought to have been delivered from it before you, even if I had had a great desire for it, and had not committed the entire determination of the matter to you.

128. But now, looking solely to your own interests you have overlooked mine. Would indeed, that you had overlooked them! that would have been agreeable to me. But you have schemed how I might be easily taken by those who wished to secure me.

129. You cannot shelter yourself here,—that the judgment of the many deceived you, and led you to think something great and wonderful about me, for I was none of your admirable and distinguished men, and even if I had happened to be so, you ought not to have preferred the opinion of the multitude to the truth.

130. For if I had never permitted you to enjoy my friendship, you might have seemed to have a reasonable pretext for giving your vote according to the report of the multitude; but if nobody knows me so well as you, if you know my mind better than my parents and those who reared me, what plea will you have so convincing as to be able to persuade such as hear you, that you have not intentionally thrust me into this danger?

131. But let this be waived; for I do not compel you to judge yourself herein: say what answer I shall give to those who accuse us?

[CHRYSOSTOM.] 132. Well, said I, I shall not proceed to those matters, before I resolve what concerns you, even if you wish me a thousand times to dispose of these charges.

133. You said that ignorance would have brought me forgiveness, and that I should have been free from all accusation if I had brought you into your present

position without knowing anything about you; but since I have not ignorantly betrayed you, but when I well understood your concerns, therefore all reasonable pretext and just defence is taken away from me.

134. But I say quite the contrary. And why? Because such things require examination, and he who is going to present one as qualified for the priesthood, ought not to be content with the report of the multitude only, but ought therewith, most of all and before all, to put his endowments to the test.

135. For when the blessed Paul says, "He must also have a good testimony from those who are without,"[28] he does not dispense with exact and strict investigation, nor lay down that as the principal sign of the acceptableness of such. For having before spoken of many things, he afterwards added this, showing that in order to such elections one must not be satisfied with this alone, but must receive it along with other things. For it often happens that the report of the multitude is false; but when careful examination precedes, no danger remains to be suspected from it.

136. On this account, after other things, he adds that which comes from those who are without. For he did not simply say, "He must have a good testimony," but he also added the other, ['from those who are without,'][29] because he wished to show that before adducing the report of those who are without, he must be carefully examined.

137. Since then I have known what pertains to you better even than your parents have, as you yourself confessed, therefore am I justly released from all blame.

[BASIL.] 138. And therefore, said he, you would not have escaped, if any one had wished to accuse you. Do you not remember to have often heard from myself of my weakness of mind, and to have learned it from my conduct? Have you not continually railed at me for pusillanimity because I easily succumbed to ordinary cares?

[CHRYSOSTOM.] 139. I remember, said I, that I have often heard these words from you, and I would not deny it. But if I ever railed at you, I did it in sport, and not in truth.

But, however, I do not at all wrangle about this now; but I ask you to show me your wonted kindness, while I wish to make mention of part of the good qualities you possess.

140. For even if you should try to convict me of speaking untruly, I shall not refrain, but shall show that you speak thus, rather as depreciating yourself, than as the truth, and I will use nothing else but your own words and deeds as witnesses for the truth of what I say.

V. CHRYSOSTOM AVOIDED THE OFFICE OUT OF LOVE TO CHRIST.

141. And first I wish to ask you this, Do you know how great the power of love is? For Christ, setting aside all the miracles which were to be wrought by the apostles, says, "By this shall men know that ye are my disciples, if ye love one another."[30]

28 1 Tim. iii. 7.

29 The words in brackets are not in the Leipzig edition.

30 John xiii. 35.

And Paul says it is the fulfilling of the law,[31] and that when this is absent no gift is profitable.[32]

142. This excellent good, the distinctive mark of the disciples of Christ, which is above all gifts, I know to be deeply implanted in your soul, and to be covered with much fruit.

[BASIL.] 143. I am indeed, said he, very careful in this matter, and I use my best endeavours in reference to the commandment, and I own it; but that I have not performed the half of it, even you will testify to me, if you dispense with speaking for favour, and mean to do honour to the truth.

[CHRYSOSTOM.] 144. I shall return to my evidences then, said I, and what I threatened, I shall now do, by showing that you would rather depreciate yourself than speak the truth. Now I will mention a thing which has just occurred, that nobody may suspect that, by telling old stories, I attempt to overshadow the truth by length of time; for oblivion[33] does not permit reliance upon things uttered by me for favour's sake.

VI. PROOF OF THE VIRTUE OF BASIL, AND OF HIS GREAT LOVE.

145. For when one of our intimate friends was falsely accused on charges of contumely and desperate conduct, and was in extreme danger, although nobody cited you, nor even he who was exposed to peril entreated you, you cast yourself into the very midst of the danger.

146. This was the deed: and to convict you also by your words, I shall recall to mind what you have said. For when some did not approve of this forwardness, though others praised and admired it, 'What am I to do?' you asked of those who criminated you, 'for I know no other way to love, than by surrendering my own life when one of my friends who is in peril has to be delivered.'

147. In other words, but with the same idea, you uttered what Christ said to his disciples when He defined the limits of perfect love: "For greater love hath no man than this," said He, "than that a man lay down his life for his friends."[34] If then greater than this cannot be found, you have attained its limit, and by what you have done, and by what you have said, you have climbed to its summit.

148. On this account I betrayed you, and on this account I manufactured that deception. Do I then persuade you that I brought you into this course, not through ill will, nor because I wished to involve you in danger, but because I knew you would be useful?

[BASIL.] 149. You think then, said he, that for the correction of one's neighbours the force of love is sufficient?

[CHRYSOSTOM]. 150. In very great part, said I, it could contribute thereto. But if you wish me also to produce examples of your prudence, I will go on to this too,

---

31 Rom. xiii. 10.

32 1 Cor. xiii. 1-3.

33 For "oblivion," the Benedictine edition reads "truth."

34 John xv. 13.

and will show that you are even more wise than you are kind.

VII. CHRYSOSTOM DID NOT AVOID ORDINATION BECAUSE HE INTENDED TO INSULT THOSE WHO DESTINED HIM FOR IT.

151. Hereupon he blushed and coloured, and said, [BASIL.] Let my concerns be dismissed now; for from the outset I never asked you for an account of these matters. But if you have anything proper to say to those who are without, I would willingly hear your words to that effect.

Therefore dismissing this shadowy contest, say, what answer shall I give to others, both to those who have honoured me, and to those who grieve for them as if they were despised?

[CHRYSOSTOM.] 152. In fine, said I, I am hastening to do this: for since my explanation to you is finished, I shall readily turn to this part of the answer. What then is their accusation, and what are the charges?

[BASIL.] They say they have been slighted by us, and shamefully wronged, because we have not accepted the honour which they desired to confer upon us.

[CHRYSOSTOM.] 153. Well, first I say this, that I am not bound to render any account of slight towards men, when by honouring them I should be compelled to offend God. Nor is it safe for those who are vexed to be annoyed about these things, but it is a great injury to them. For I think that such as are set apart to God, and look to Him alone, ought to conduct themselves so piously, as not to account it an insult, even if they should be dishonoured a thousand times.

154. But that I have not dared to do this even in thought, is manifest from hence; that if I had come to this degree through folly and love of glory, as you have often said some even slanderously affirm, I ought to be reckoned by my accusers with such as have perpetrated the greatest wrong, as having despised men who were great and worthy of admiration, and besides, my benefactors.[35] For if to wrong those who have not wronged us is deserving of punishment, what vengeance does it not deserve to repay the contrary to those who have chosen of their own accord to honour us? (since nobody can say that those who have been favoured in little or much by me have made any return for such benefits).[36]

155. But if I never allowed this to enter my mind, but on other advice declined the heavy burden, why, while omitting to forgive, even if they do not consent to approve, do they condemn me because I spared my own soul?

156. For I was so far from insulting the men in question, that I should say I have honoured them by my refusal. And do not be surprised if what I have been saying

---

35 According to another reading:—'For if I had come to this degree through folly or vain glory, as you have often said some men slanderously affirm, I should be one of the greatest wrongdoers, as having despised men who were great and worthy of admiration, and besides, my benefactors.'

36 There is another reading of this involved sentence: 'For if to wrong those who have not wronged us is deserving of punishment, how ought we to honour those who have chosen of their own accord to honour us? (for nobody can say that those who have been favoured in little or much by me, have made any return for such benefits). What vengeance would it not deserve to repay them with the contrary!'

is paradoxical, for I shall supply a speedy solution of it.

VIII. Chrysostom even freed his friends from blame by his flight.

157. For if not all, yet those to whom it is a pleasure to speak evil, would then have had many grounds to cherish suspicion and to talk of me if I had been ordained, and of those who elected me. Thus,—that they regard wealth, that they admire splendour of rank, and that because they were flattered by me they brought me to this honour: I cannot say whether any one would have suspected even this—that they had been persuaded by bribes.

158. Moreover, (they would have said) "Christ called fishermen and tentmakers to this dignity;[37] but these despise such as are supported by their daily labour,[38] whereas if anyone embraces external learning, and is supported in idleness, they accept and admire him. Why forsooth, have they overlooked those who have endured abundant drudgery for the service of the church, but all at once exalted to this honour one who never tasted labours of this sort, and wasted all his youth in the vain pursuit of external learning?"

159. This and more than this they would have said, had I received the office; but not now; for all pretext of accusation is cut off from them. Nor can they accuse me of flattery or them of venality, save such as may merely wish to rave.

160. For how should he who flattered and bribed in order to obtain an honour, leave it to others, just when he might have received it? This would be as if a man who had expended much labour on a piece of land that its crop might bow down with weight of fruit, and the presses overflow with wine, after innumerable toils, and much expenditure of money, should relinquish to others the produce of his crops just when he ought to reap his corn and gather his vintage.

161. You see that even if what was said was far from the truth, yet still those who desired to slander would have a pretext, as that they had not made the election with just judgment and reason. But I have not allowed them now either to gape, or even to open their mouth. Such otherwise would have been their sayings at the outset, and more than these.

162. But after receiving the ministry, I should not have been competent to defend myself daily against those who uttered accusations, even if I had done everything blamelessly: not to say that I must have had many faults, in consequence of inexperience, and of my youth: but now I have relieved them of this accusation, whereas then I should have involved them in countless reproaches.

163. What would they not have said? "They have committed to thoughtless youths such great and admirable affairs; they have defiled the flock of God; Christian interests have become a sport and a laughing-stock." But now, "all iniquity shall stop her mouth;"[39] and if they should also say these things about you, never-

---

37 Matt. iv. 9; Acts xviii. 3.

38 Luke v. 27.

39 Ps. cvii. 42.

theless you will speedily teach them by your deeds, that men ought not to estimate wisdom by age, nor to test the elder by his grey head;[40] nor wholly to exclude the young man from this ministry, but the novice;[41] and there is a great difference between the two.

---

40 Wisd. iv. 8, 9.

41 1 Tim. iii. 6; iv. 12.

Book III.[42]

I. They who suspected him of declining the Priesthood through arrogance, injured their own reputation.

[Chrysostom.] 164. As it regards my contempt for those who have honoured me, and my having evaded the honour because I did not wish to put them to shame, I might say what I have already said. But I will now try to the best of my ability to make it plain to you that I have not been puffed up with any arrogance.

165. If the acceptance of a generalship or of a kingdom had been proposed to me, and I had then entertained this sentiment, this might reasonably have been suspected; or rather, no one would then have condemned me for arrogance, but all would for insanity. But when the priesthood was within my reach, a thing which is as far above a kingdom, as the distance between flesh and spirit, who will venture to accuse me of contemning it?

166. And is it not absurd that those who reject trifles should be charged with being unreasonable,—and yet to deliver from accusations of folly those who act thus in regard to things much more excellent, and to subject them to charges of vanity? It is as though one should accuse him who looked with contempt upon a herd of oxen and would not be a herdsman, not of vanity but of the loss of reason, and should say that he who would not accept the government of all the world, and be lord of universal armies, was puffed up with pride, and not that he was insane.

167. But it is assuredly not so; nor do they who say thus, slander me more than themselves. For only to imagine that it is possible for human nature to despise that authority, is a token of the honour in which those who say so, hold the matter; for if they did not think it to be among ordinary things and such as are not of much account, it would not have occurred to them to suspect this.

168. In reference to the honour of angels, why has no one ever ventured to suspect and to say it is because of pride that the human soul does not aspire to attain to the dignity of their nature? For we imagine something grand concerning those powers, and this does not allow us to believe that man could conceive of anything greater than their honour.

169. So that one would more justly accuse of pride those who make this charge against me; for they would never have suspected this of others, if they had not first depreciated the matter as of no account.

170. But if they say I have done this with a view to glory, they will be convicted of coming into collision, and of openly contradicting themselves; for I do not know what other language they would have devised in preference to this if they had

---

42 Chapters I. to XI. are indicated at the head of the ordinary Greek text. The rest are added in the Latin versions.

wished to free me from accusations of vain glory.

II. He did not avoid it through vain glory.

171. If such a kind of love had ever possessed me, I ought rather to have accepted than avoided the office. Wherefore? Because it would have brought me much glory. The fact that one of my age, who had recently abandoned worldly pursuits, should so suddenly be deemed worthy of admiration by all, as to be honoured in preference to such as have spent their whole time in these labours, and to receive more suffrages than they, would have persuaded all men to surmise something great and admirable concerning me, and would have caused me to be reverenced and respected.

172. But now, excepting a few, the greater portion of the Church does not know me even by name: so that it is not plain to all that I have refused, but only to a few; nor do they, I fancy, know it certainly; and perhaps even of them, many think I have not been elected at all, or have been passed over after election, because I seemed to be unsuitable, and not that I have declined of my own accord.

III. If he had desired glory he would rather have chosen it.

[BASIL.] 173. But they who know the truth will be surprised.

[CHRYSOSTOM.] And they, you say, speak against me as vain-glorious and haughty! From whence then am I to hope for praise? From the many? But they do not know the truth. Well then, from the few? But here also the matter is perverted into something against me; because you have come here for nothing else than to learn what answer ought to be made to them.

174. And why do I now argue so specially on their account? Because if all had known the truth they ought not to have thus condemned me for pride and love of glory: wait a little, and you will know this clearly; and not only this, but also that no small danger is incurred, both by those who make this venture (if indeed there are such men, as I am not convinced there are), and also by those who cherish suspicion on other points.

IV. The Priesthood is something tremendous; and the priesthood of the New Testament is a much more solemn business than that of the Old Law.

175. The priestly office is discharged upon earth, but holds the rank of heavenly things; and very rightly so. For not man, nor angel, nor archangel, nor any other created power, but the Paraclete himself, instituted this order, and induced those who yet abode in the flesh to make manifest the ministry of angels. Wherefore it behoves him that is consecrated to be as pure as one who stands in heaven itself among those powers.

176. Awful indeed, and most terrible, were those things which were prior to grace, such as the bells, the pomegranates, the stones of the breastplate and of the ephod, the mitre, the turban, the long robe, the plate of gold, the holy of holies, and

the great silence therein;[43] but if any one should examine the things which pertain to grace, he will find that while they are small they are fearful and most terrible; and here also it was true which was spoken concerning the law, namely, that what was made glorious is not glorified in this respect, by reason of the glory which excelleth.[44]

177. For when you behold the Lord sacrificed and prostrate, and the priest standing over the sacrifice and praying, and all stained with that precious blood, do you then suppose you are among men, and standing upon earth? are you not immediately transported to heaven? and casting out every carnal idea from your soul, do you not with naked soul and pure mind contemplate things which are in heaven? O the marvel! O the love of God to man! He who sits with the Father on high is at that moment held in the hands of all, and gives Himself to those who are willing to embrace and to receive Him; and then all do this by the eyes [of faith[45]]. Do these things appear to you to be worthy to be despised, or to be such that any one can be lifted up against them?

178. Do you wish from another marvel to perceive its pre-eminent sacredness? Picture Elijah to your eyes, and an immense crowd standing around, and the sacrifice lying upon the stones, and all the rest in silence and great stillness, and the prophet alone praying: then suddenly the flame from heaven rushing upon the sacrifice.[46] Marvellous were these things and full of all terror.

179. Pass from thence to what is now performed, and you will see, not only marvellous things, but things which transcend all terror. For the priest stands, not bearing fire, but the Holy Ghost; and he makes supplication for a long time, not that any flame sent from above may consume what is before him, but that grace alighting upon the sacrifice may thereby enkindle the souls of all, and render them brighter than silver purified by fire.

180. Will not he be exceedingly mad and out of his mind, who can despise this most tremendous rite? or are you ignorant that the human soul would never have endured that sacrificial fire, but all would have utterly perished, unless the help of God's grace had been great?

V. THE GREAT AUTHORITY AND HONOUR OF PRIESTS.

181. For if any one consider what it is, for him that is a man, and still composed of flesh and blood, to be able to approach that blessed and immortal nature, he will then see clearly what honour the grace of the Spirit has vouchsafed to priests; for by them these things are performed, and others not inferior to them, both as regards our dignity and our salvation.

182. For those who dwell upon earth and make their abode therein, have been commissioned to dispense things which are in heaven, and have received an au-

---

43 Exod. 28.

44 2 Cor. iii. 10.

45 The words 'of faith' are not in the Leipsic text.

46 1 Kings 18.

thority such as God has not given either to angels or to archangels. For it has not been said to them, "Whatsoever ye shall bind upon earth shall be bound also in heaven; and whatsoever ye shall loose, shall be loosed."[47]

183. Those who rule upon earth, indeed, have authority to bind, but bodies only; whereas this bond takes hold of the soul itself, and reaches heaven; what priests execute below, God ratifies above, and the Master confirms the judgment of his servants.

184. And what is this, but that he has given them all heavenly authority? For he says, "Whose sins ye remit, they are remitted, and whose sins ye retain, they are retained."[48] What authority can be greater than this? "All judgment hath the Father committed to the Son;"[49] but I see that they have been entrusted with all this by the Son, as if they had already been translated to heaven, and had got beyond human nature, and were released from our affections, to so great power have they been raised.

185. Moreover, if a king should confer upon one of his subjects this honour, — to cast into prison whom he would, and to release them again; the man would be envied and respected by all. But he who receives from God an authority as much greater as heaven is more precious than earth, and souls than bodies, seems to some men to have received so small an honour, that it is possible even to suppose that one of those entrusted therewith will despise the gift.

186. Away with such madness! for it is transparent madness to despise so great a power, without which we can acquire neither salvation nor the good things which have been promised us.

187. For if no one can enter the kingdom of heaven, except he be regenerate by water and the Spirit;[50] and if he who does not eat the flesh of the Lord, and drink his blood, is excluded from eternal life;[51] and if all these things are accomplished only by those holy hands, the priest's I mean, how will any one be able without them to escape the fire of Gehenna, or to obtain the crowns which are in store?

188. For it is verily these who have been entrusted with the pains of the spiritual birth, and have had committed to them that nativity of ours which is by baptism; through these we are clothed with Christ, and are united with[52] the Son of God, and become members of that Blessed Head.

189. Wherefore, they would not only be more justly venerated by us than rulers and kings, but more honoured than our fathers; for the one begat us by blood and the will of the flesh;[53] but the others are the authors of our nativity which is from

47 Matth. xviii. 18.

48 John xx. 23.

49 John v. 22.

50 John iii. 5.

51 John vi. 53.

52 Another reading gives 'buried with.'

53 John i. 13.

God; that blessed regeneration, true liberty, and adoption according to grace.[54]

VI. PRIESTS THE MINISTERS OF GOD'S GREATEST GIFTS.

190. The priests of the Jews had authority to take away leprosy of body, or rather, by no means to take it away, but only to examine such as had been freed from it;[55] and you know how the office of priests was then contended for. But these have received authority not over leprosy of body, but impurity of soul, not to examine when it has been taken away, but altogether to remove it.

191. Therefore such as despise them, are much more criminal, and are worthy of a greater vengeance than those who were associated with Dathan; for, although they affected a dignity which did not appertain to them, they, notwithstanding, still entertained a certain admiring opinion in regard to it, and this they proved by pursuing it with so much eagerness: but these, when the office has been adorned more excellently, and has received so great a development, have displayed their audacity in a contrary manner, but to a much greater degree than those did.[56]

192. For as regards the amount of contempt, it is not the same thing to pounce upon an honour which does not pertain to you, and to despise it; but the one is as much beyond the other, as the interval between loathing and admiring.

193. What soul then is so base as to slight such good things? No one, I should say, unless it were subject to a demoniacal impulse.

194. But I come back again to where I started from. Not in chastising only, but in benefiting, God has given to priests a greater power than that of our natural parents: and the two differ as much as the present and the future life.

195. For the one beget us unto this life, and the others unto that. Neither can our parents avert from us bodily death, nor repulse impending disease; but these frequently save the soul when it is afflicted and ready to perish,—securing to some a milder chastisement, and not permitting others to fall in any degree; not by teaching only, and admonition, but also by aiding them through prayer.

196. Nor only when they regenerate us, have they authority to forgive sins, but also (they have authority to forgive) such sins as come afterwards: for, he says, "Is any sick among you? let him call for the presbyters of the church, and let them pray over him, anointing him with oil in the name of the Lord; and the prayer of faith shall save him that is sick, and the Lord shall raise him up; and if he has committed sins, they shall be forgiven him."[57]

197. Moreover, natural parents, if their children should come into collision with any of their superiors and those who have great influence, cannot benefit them at all: but priests have reconciled, not rulers, nor kings, but God himself oftentimes when angry with them.

198. After this, will any one still venture to condemn me for arrogance? After

---

54 1 Cor. iv. 5; Philem. 10; Tit. iii. 5; John viii. 36; Gal. v. 1, iv. 5.

55 Lev. xiv. 1-7.

56 Numb. 16.

57 James v. 14, 15.

what has been said, I imagine, so strong a pious affection will control the souls of those who hear, that they will no longer condemn for arrogance and venturesomeness those who evade the honour, but those who come forward of their own accord, and are eager to get possession of it for themselves.

199. For if those who have had committed to them the government of cities, when they have not happened to be wise and very watchful, have overturned their cities and ruined themselves; of how much power, think you, both in himself and from on high, to keep himself from sin, has he need, whose lot it is to beautify the Bride of Christ?

VII. S. Paul was awestruck when he contemplated the magnitude of this office.

200. No man loved Christ more than Paul, no one displayed a greater zeal than he, nobody has been counted worthy of more grace; and yet, after all this, he still fears and trembles, as well about this presidency, as about those who were presided over by him: for, said he, "I fear, lest, as the serpent deceived Eve, so your minds should be corrupted from the simplicity which is in Christ."[58] And again, "I was with you in fear and in much trembling."[59]

201. A man who had been caught up to the third heaven, and had participated in the unspeakable things of God, and endured as many deaths as he lived days after he believed in Christ! a man who would not even use the authority which had been given him from Christ, lest any one of those who believed should be stumbled!

202. If now he who went beyond the ordinances of Christ, and by no means sought his own advantage, but that of those whom he ruled over, was always so fearful, when he regarded the greatness of his rule, what shall we do who often seek our own, and who not merely do not go beyond the commands of Christ, but for the most part transgress them? "Who is weak," says he, "and I am not weak? Who is stumbled, and I burn not?"[60]

203. Such a one ought the priest to be, or rather, only such; for these things are little, and even nothing to what I am about to say.

204. And what is that? "I would," says he, "that I might be accursed from Christ, for my brethren, my kinsmen after the flesh."[61] If anybody could utter such a speech, if anybody had the soul which is equal to such a prayer, he would be justly accused if he drew back.

205. But if anyone should lack so much virtue,—as I do,—he would be justly odious, not when he drew back, but when he accepted.

206. If an election to some military dignity were about to take place, and those who had the power to grant the office, dragged forward a brazier, or a shoemaker, or some such artizan, and committed an army to him, I should not praise the un-

---

58 2 Cor. xi. 3.

59 1 Cor. ii. 3.

60 2 Cor. xi. 29.

61 Rom. ix. 3.

happy man, unless he fled, and did everything to avoid thrusting himself into so much evident mischief.[62]

207. If it suffices simply to be called a pastor and to perform the business as it may happen, and there be no danger in this, let whoso will accuse me of vain-glory; but if it behoves him who accepts this responsibility to have much understanding, and before understanding, great grace from God, and uprightness of conduct, and purity of life, and virtue more than human, deprive me not of pardon if I wish not to perish without cause and in vain.

208. If also any one brought me a great ship, full of rowers, and laden with a precious cargo, and then stationed me at the helm, and bade me cross the Ægean or the Tyrrhene sea, I should recoil at the first word; and if any one asked me why, I should say, "Lest I should sink the ship."

VIII. HE WHO ENTERS UPON THIS OFFICE IS OFTEN LED INTO SIN UNLESS HE BE A VERY NOBLE-MINDED MAN.

209. Where the loss extends only to property then, and the danger to bodily death, no one will lay any charge to those who use much forethought; but where the destiny of those who are shipwrecked is, not to fall into this sea, but into the abyss of fire; and the death which awaits them is not that which divides the soul from the body, but that which along with this dismisses it to eternal punishment, why here, do you rage and hate because I did not throw myself headlong into so great mischief? Do not, I pray and entreat you.

210. I know my own soul, which is feeble and weak. I know the greatness of that ministry, and the extreme difficulty of the thing.

211. Greater waves than those with which the winds disturb the ocean, agitate the soul of him that becomes a priest.

IX. THE MAN WHO IS NOT OF A NOBLE SPIRIT IS ENSNARED BY VAIN-GLORY, AND ITS ATTENDANT EVILS.

And first of all, there is that most terrible rock of vain-glory, which is more dreadful than that of those (Sirens) of whom the mythologists tell such wonderful stories.

212. For many who have sailed by that have been able to avoid it in safety, but this is so difficult to me that I am not able to get clear of the peril even now, when no necessity at all urges me towards the whirlpool. If any one should commit this oversight to me, it would only be as if he bound my hands behind me, and delivered me to the wild beasts which inhabit that rock, to rend me day by day.

213. And what are these wild beasts? Wrath, dejection, envy, contention, slanders, accusations, falsehood, hypocrisy, plots, ill-will towards such as have done no wrong, pleasure in the indecorous acts of one's fellow ministers, sorrow over their successes, love of praises, lust of honour, (which most of all casts down the human soul headlong), doctrine which causes delight, sordid flatteries, ignoble time-servings, contempt for the poor, court to the rich, honours without reason, and favours hurtful, bringing perils to those who give and those who take them, servile fear,

---

62 For "I should not praise," some read "They would not praise."

such as befits only the most worthless of slaves, abandonment of outspokenness, abundance of humility in appearance, but truth nowhere, rebukes and censures absent, or rather, directed against the low beyond measure, while to such as are surrounded with influence one dare not open his lips.

214. All these wild beasts, and more than these that rock supports, and those who are once caught by them are inevitably dragged into such servitude, that oftentimes, and even to please women, they do many things which it is not well to mention.

215. The divine law has excluded these from the ministry, but they strive to force themselves into it; and when they cannot prevail in the least by themselves they accomplish everything by means of others; and they are arrayed in so much power that they can appoint or eject whatever priests they will.

216. Things are upside down; for that may be seen to have happened which agrees with the proverb: "Subjects govern princes," and I would they were men who do it, but it is also women to whom it is enjoined not to teach.[63] Why do I say to teach?—the blessed Paul has not even permitted them to speak in the Church.[64] But I have heard somebody say, that they enjoyed so much liberty of speech as to rebuke the prelates of the churches, and censure them more sharply than masters their domestics.

217. However, let no one suppose that I subject all to the charges which have been mentioned: for there are some, there are many, who are superior to these entanglements, yea more than are caught in them.

X. THE PRIESTHOOD NOT THE CAUSE OF THESE EVILS, BUT OUR OWN DULLNESS.

218. Nevertheless, I would not blame the priestly office for these evils. Let me not be so infatuated as that. For no men of understanding say that the sword is to blame for murder, or wine for drunkenness, or power for insolence, or courage for unreasonable daring; but that they are to blame who do not use as they ought the gifts which God has given; and them they punish.

219. Therefore the priestly office will justly accuse us, if we do not rightly administer it. For it is not to blame for the evils which have been mentioned, but we who have profaned it with as many pollutions as we could, by conferring it upon such persons as came in our way, who had neither become acquainted with their own souls, nor considered the gravity of the office, but readily accepted what was offered them, and when they came to the work, being clouded by inexperience, they overwhelmed with a myriad evils the people entrusted to them.

220. This is the very thing almost which must have happened to me, if God had not suddenly delivered me from those dangers,—thus sparing both his own Church and my soul.

221. Whence, tell me, do you think so great troubles are generated in the Churches? I do not think they come from any where else, than from the choice and

---

63 1 Tim. ii. 12.

64 1 Cor. xiv. 34, 35.

election of prelates rashly and by chance.

222. For the head ought to be the strongest, that it may be able to superintend and reduce to order all the evil exhalations from beneath which arise from the rest of the body; but when it happens to be weak in itself and incompetent to repel those pestiferous attacks, it becomes even feebler than it is, and ruins the rest of the body as well as itself.

223. That this might not now come to pass, God has kept my feet in the rank which I occupied from the beginning.

224. There are very many other things besides those which have been mentioned, Basil, which a priest ought to have, and I have not, and before others, this: his soul must be altogether purified from the desire of the office.

225. For if he should perchance incline too eagerly to this post, when he attains it he kindles a yet more violent flame, and being taken by force, he will suffer a myriad of mischiefs in order to hold it fast, even though it should be necessary to flatter, or to suffer what is ignoble and unworthy, or to spend abundance of wealth.

226. For that some have filled the churches with murders, and made cities desolate, when contending for this position, I now pass over, lest I should seem to say what is incredible to any.

227. But I think one ought to have so much reverence for the matter, as to avoid the charge at the outset; and after having entered upon it, not to wait the judgment of others if any fault should be committed sufficient to call for deposition, but to anticipate them and retire from office; for thus would mercy be likely to be obtained from God. To cling to the office in an unseemly manner, is to deprive oneself of all pardon, and to enkindle yet more the anger of God, by adding a second and a worse offence.

XI. THE LUST OF DOMINATION IS TO BE CAST OUT OF THE SOUL OF A PRIEST.

But no one can always hold out; for fearful, truly fearful is the coveting of this honour.

228. I speak not in opposition to the blessed Paul, but thoroughly in harmony with his words;—and what says he? "If a man desire the office of a bishop, he desireth a good work."[65] Now I do not say it is a fearful thing to desire the work, but authority and power.

229. And this desire I think should be expelled from the soul with all earnestness, and not suffered to prevail over it even at the outset, in order that one may be allowed to do everything with freedom.

230. For he who desires not to be exhibited as one who has this authority, does not fear removal from it; and not fearing this, he would be able to do everything with the freedom befitting Christians.

231. Whereas, those who fear and tremble lest they should be deposed, endure a bitter servitude and one full of all evils, and are oftentimes driven to offend against both God and men.

232. Now the mind ought not to be thus affected; but as in wars we see the

---

65 1 Tim. iii. 1.

nobler soldiers fighting willingly and falling manfully; so they who attain to this ministry, should be both consecrated and removed from office in a manner befitting Christian men, knowing that such a removal brings a crown not inferior to that of the office.

233. For when any one suffers something of this kind for not enduring anything unbecoming or unworthy of that dignity, he procures punishment for such as unjustly depose him, and a greater reward for himself. "Blessed," says our Lord, "are ye, when men shall revile and persecute you, and shall say all manner of evil against you falsely for my sake. Rejoice, and be exceeding glad; for great is your reward in heaven."[66]

234. And these things happen when any one is expelled by those of his own order, either through envy, or in favour of others, or through enmity, or from any other motive which is not right.

235. Now when it befalls one to suffer thus from such as are opposed to him, I think it does not require a word to show the profit which by their wickedness they confer upon him.

236. Therefore we must every way attend to and carefully search into this,— that no spark of that desire be secretly smouldering anywhere.

237. It were to be wished also, that those who were at first free from this affection, should be able to avoid it when they come into office; but if, before attaining the honour, any one cherishes in himself this dreadful and obstinate wild beast, it is impossible to say into what a furnace he will throw himself after he has attained it.

238. Now I, (and think not that I would ever lie to you in underrating myself), possessed very much of this desire; and this, with other things, frightened me no little, and put me to flight.

239. For as they who cherish human love, endure a severer torment of passion, while suffered to be near the objects of their affection, but throw aside their madness when they remove as far as possible from those they long after; so those who desire this office find the evil intolerable while they are near it; but extinguish the desire along with the expectation, when they cease to hope for it.

XII. A PRIEST OUGHT TO BE A VERY WISE MAN.

240. This one motive then, is not a slight one; but if it had happened to be alone by itself, it would have been enough to keep me from the dignity.

241. There is however, another to be now added not less than this; and what is it? That a priest must be sober-minded, and clear-sighted, and have a myriad of eyes in every direction; as one who lives not for himself alone but for so great a multitude.

242. But I am sluggish, and remiss, and scarcely sufficient for my own salvation, as even you would confess, who most of all are eager to hide my failings, through love to me.

243. Speak not to me here of fasting and watching, of sleeping on the ground, and other hard discipline of the body; for you know how far I come short in these things; and even if they had been regulated to a nicety, would have been unable,

---

66 Matt. v. 11, 12.

with my present sluggishness, to benefit me in the least in respect to such a post of authority.

244. Such things might confer advantage upon a man who is shut up in some cell, and who only concerns himself about his own interests; but when a man is divided among so great a multitude, and has inherited the private cares of all that are under his direction, what appreciable gain to their improvement would he be able to contribute, unless he were endowed with a robust and vigorous soul?

XIII. OTHER REQUIREMENTS BESIDES ABSTINENCE ARE LOOKED FOR IN A PRIEST.

245. Wonder not if in connection with such endurance I require another test of excellence of soul.

246. For, we see that to be indifferent about meats and drinks and a soft bed, is no hard matter to many, and especially to such as are rudely constituted, and have been thus trained from early youth; and in many others, discipline of body and custom mitigate the severity of these performances. But contempt, insolence, harsh speeches, and sarcasms from inferiors, whether rashly or righteously uttered, and rebukes vainly and idly spoken by rulers and the ruled,—it is not many who can endure, but only one or two here and there.

247. And you may see those who are strong for the former, so agitated by the latter, that they are more furious than savage wild beasts.

248. We should keep out of the enclosures of the priesthood men of this sort especially. That a minister should not obstinately repudiate food, nor go barefoot, would be no injury whatever to the community of the Church; but a furious temper causes great misfortune both to its possessor and his neighbours.

249. There is no threatening from God against such as do not do the things referred to; but they who are angry without reason are menaced with Gehenna and the fire of Gehenna.

250. As therefore, the lover of vain-glory adds fresh fuel to the fire when he undertakes the oversight of a multitude; so he who while alone or in company with a few is unable to control his temper but is easily carried away, when he is entrusted with the rule of an entire congregation, like some wild beast goaded on every side by myriads, will never be able to abide in peace himself, and will scatter innumerable evils among those who are committed to him.

XIV. MENTAL PURITY AND ACTIVITY HINDERED BY NOTHING SO MUCH AS BY INORDINATE ANGER.

251. Nothing so bedims the transparency of the mind, and the perspicacity of the understanding, as wrath when it is inordinate and impetuous.

252. 'For this,' says one, 'destroys even the prudent.'[67] For the eye of the soul being darkened as in some conflict by night, is incapable of discerning friends from foes, and the unworthy from the honourable, but handles them all in turn in the same manner, and if some harm must be suffered, anything is readily endured for

---

67 Prov. xv. 1.

the sake of performing what the soul takes pleasure in.

253. The fire of anger is a sort of pleasure, and governs the soul more sternly than pleasure, by utterly turning upside down its healthy condition. It easily hurries a man into caprice, and untimely enmities, and unreasonable hatred; and it constantly causes the commission of offences rashly and idly, and forces the doing and saying of many other similar things, because the soul is swept along by the greatviolence of passion, and has nothing whereon to fix its strength, and resist the impulse.

254. [BASIL] I shall suffer you to dissimulate no further; for who knows not, (said he) how far removed you are from this infirmity?

255. [CHRYSOSTOM.] Why then, my good friend, said I, do you wish to bring me nearer the fire, and to rouse up the wild beast which is quiet? Do you not know, that I have done this by no virtue of my own, but through love of retirement? He that is thus constituted, is able to escape the conflagration which follows, while he remains devoted to himself, or associates merely with one or two friends, but not when he falls into such an abyss of cares.

256. For then he drags not only himself, but many others with him to the brink of ruin, and renders them more indifferent to all concern for propriety. For it generally happens, that the majority of those who are governed, regard the manners of their rulers as a sort of model image, and make themselves like them. How then can he appease their passions, who is swollen with anger himself? Who among the multitude would straightway desire to be moderate, if he saw his ruler angry?

257. For it is utterly impossible for the failings of priests to be hidden; but the very least become immediately manifest.

258. An athlete, so long as he remains at home, and contends with nobody, may conceal it even though he is very weak; but when he strips for the conflict, he is easily found out. And some men who live a private and inactive life, have their seclusion as a veil over their faults; but when they come into the arena, they are forced to strip off solitude as a garment, and to show their naked souls to all men by means of their outward movements.

259. As therefore, their right deeds have profited many by provoking them to equal zeal; so have their shortcomings made men more indifferent to the practice of virtue, and rendered them sluggish in their endeavours after what is excellent. Wherefore the beauty of his soul ought to shine forth in every direction, that it may at once both gladden and enlighten the souls of the beholders.

260. For the faults of ordinary men, which are as though committed in the dark, ruin only those who perpetrate them; but the vices of a man who is conspicuous and known to many, inflict a common injury upon all, making those more remiss who have relaxed in their strivings after good, and rendering capricious those who wish to give heed to themselves.

261. And apart from these things, the faults of the obscure, even if they come into notice, are punished with no remarkable punishment; but those who are seated upon this pinnacle of honour, are, in the first place, manifest to all men, and in the next place, if they fail in the smallest matters, that which is small seems great to others; for all men estimate an offence, not by the measure of the action, but by the dignity of him who sins.

262. The priest must be fortified as though by adamantine armour, and must watch on every side with constant zeal and perpetual vigilance in respect to his life, lest any one should find some naked and unguarded spot and inflict a fatal wound. For all who stand around are prepared to smite and cast him down,—not merely his enemies and foes, but many even of those who profess to be his friends.

263. The souls which ought to be selected therefore, are such as God's grace once manifested the bodies of his saints to be in the Babylonian furnace. Faggot, and pitch, and tow, are not the fuel of this fire, but things more dreadful far than they; because it is not a material fire which threatens them, but the all-devouring flame of calumny surrounds them, rising on every side, assailing them and putting their life to a severer test than the fire then did the bodies of those young men. When therefore it finds the slightest trace of stubble, it rapidly seizes upon it, and consumes the vitiated part, and utterly scorches and blackens with smoke all the rest of the edifice, even though it should be brighter than the sunbeams.

264. So long as the life of a priest is well ordered in every way, it is invulnerable to plots; but if he overlook ever so little, as easily happens, since he is but a man, and is crossing the devious ocean of this life, he derives no advantage from the rest of his good deeds, by their enabling him to escape the mouths of accusers, for that little fault overshadows all besides. All men will judge the priest, not as one arrayed in flesh, nor as one inheriting human nature, but as an angel, and one delivered from remaining infirmity.

265. And just as all men fear and flatter a tyrant so long as he is in power, because they cannot depose him; but when they see things going contrary, lay aside their hypocritical honour, and those who shortly before were his friends, suddenly become his foes and enemies, and searching out all his weak points, attack him and get rid of his government; so is it with a priest: when they who a little before, and while he was in power, honoured and served him, find some little failing, they speedily make ready to depose him, not as a tyrant only, but something even worse than this.

266. As the former fears those who are the guardians of his body, so the latter most dreads those who are near him and minister with him. For no others desire his office so much as these, and know his affairs so well; and since they are near him, if anything occurs they are aware of it before others; and they are able to command belief when they slander, and by magnifying trifles, they can take him captive whom they have maligned. The apostolic saying is reversed; "If one member suffers, all the rest rejoice; and if one member is honoured, all the members suffer:"[68] —unless indeed a man has so much piety as to be able to withstand everything.

267. Are you then for sending me into such a war? and do you think my soul equal to so varied and multiform a conflict? Whence and from whom have you learnt this? For if God has so decided, show me the oracle, and I obey. But if you cannot, but arrive at the decision by human opinion, free yourself at length from the deceit in which you have been involved. For, as to what concerns me, it is but just that I should rather be persuaded by myself than by others; inasmuch as "no man

---

68 Compare 1 Cor. xii. 26.

knoweth the things of a man but the spirit of a man which is in him."[69]

268. I fancy you are now persuaded by what I say, even if you were not before, that I should render both myself and those who appointed me ridiculous, if, after receiving this office, I returned again, greatly injured, to the course of life which I now pursue.

269. For not merely calumny, but something much more violent than calumny—the longing after this office, is wont to arm many against him that holds it.

270. And as covetous children bear with impatience the old age of their parents, so also some of these, when they see the priestly office held by any one for a long time,—since it is not proper to destroy him,—are eager to remove him from his post, all coveting to be appointed instead of him, and each expecting that the appointment will be conveyed to himself.

XV. ANOTHER KIND OF CONFLICT WHICH IS FRAUGHT WITH PERIL.

271. Do you wish me to show you another aspect of this conflict, and one fraught with ten thousand dangers? Go and contemplate the public festivals, at which especially it is the custom for elections to ecclesiastical offices to be made; and you will see the priest lying under as many accusations as is the number of those who are subject to him.

272. For all who have influence upon the bestowment of the honour, are divided into many parties; and you will not see the council of presbyters of one accord, either with each other or with him that has been chosen bishop; but every one stands by himself, one selecting this man and another that.

273. Now the reason is, they do not all look to the one thing to which alone they ought to look—excellence of spirit. But there are other considerations which favour an appointment to this honour. Thus, one says, 'Let him be appointed, because he is of an excellent family;' and another, 'Because he is possessed of great wealth, and would not need to be supported out of the revenues of the Church;' and another, 'Because he has ventured among us from our enemies' One is zealous to promote in honour before others, the man that is intimately acquainted with him; another, him that is related to him by family ties; and another, the man that flatters him. Nobody will look out for the man that is qualified, nor make any trial of soul.

274. Now I am so far from thinking these to be trustworthy means for testing any priest, that even if one manifested great piety, which contributes not a little in regard to that office, I should not venture at once to judge him by that, unless in addition to his piety he was a man of much understanding.

275. For I have known many who have always exercised restraint upon themselves, and have been consumed by fastings, who while they could be alone, and attend to their own affairs, were well-pleasing to God, and every day made no small addition to their wisdom; but when they came into the crowd, and were compelled to correct the ignorance of the multitude, some of them were from the outset unequal to so great a business, and others, while forced to persevere, yet, renouncing their former strictness, injured themselves to the utmost, and benefited others not in the least.

69 1 Cor. ii. 11.

276. But again, even if one had passed all his time in the lowest order of the ministry, and had reached the furthest limit of old age, I should not elevate him to a higher office simply because I reverenced his old age. What, if even at that time of life, he should continue still unqualified?

277. I say not this now, because I wish to dishonour the grey head, nor as laying down a law that those who come from the monastic circle should be altogether excluded from this dignity, (for it has happened that many who have come from that body have been illustrious in this office); but because I was anxious to show, that if neither piety by itself, nor advanced age, would suffice to prove worthy of the priesthood a man who had entered it, the previous considerations would hardly do so.

278. But other reasons are added, and yet more absurd. For some are enrolled with the clerical order, that they may not range themselves among opponents; and others on account of their malice, and that they may not do great mischief through being overlooked.

279. Could anything be more lawless than this? Men who are bad and full of innumerable evils, have services done them for the very things for which they ought to be punished; and ascend to the priestly dignity for things because whereof they should not be allowed to cross the threshold of the church!

280. Tell me then, shall we still inquire the reason of the wrath of God, when we expose things so holy and venerable to be defiled by bad men and men who deserve nothing? For when some are entrusted with control over what is not at all adapted to them, and others with what is far beyond their proper ability, they make the church to differ in nowise from the Euripus.

281. Formerly, indeed, I ridiculed worldly princes, because they conferred their honours not out of regard to virtue in men's souls, but from regard to wealth, and number of years, and human pre-eminence; but when I heard that this unreasonableness had intruded upon our practices, I no longer made the matter of so much account.

282. For what wonder is it that men of the world, who desire the praise of the multitude, and do everything for money, should sin in this way, when such as profess to be delivered from all these things do no better than they do, but if they have a dispute about heavenly things, after consulting as though about acres of land or some other such matter, rashly take common men and appoint them over affairs like those for which the only-begotten Son of God refused not to vacate his own glory, and to become a man, and to take the form of a servant, and to be spit upon, and to be buffeted, and to die in the flesh a most ignominious death?[70]

283. And they stop not even at these things, but they add others still more absurd; for they not only decide in favour of the unworthy, they reject those who are qualified. For, as though the security of the Church must needs be injured both ways, or as if the former cause did not suffice to inflame the wrath of God, they join on to it a second not less pernicious. For I think both the excluding of the useful, and the thrusting in of the useless, are equally to be dreaded. And this is the result,—the flock of Christ can no where find either consolation or refreshment.

---

70 Compare Phil. ii. 7, 8.

284. Do not these things deserve innumerable thunderbolts, and a more vehement Gehenna than that with which we are menaced? But yet, He who willeth not the death of the sinner, that he may be converted and live,[71] endures and bears such evils.[72] How we ought to admire his love to man, and be astounded at his mercy! They who are Christ's, ruin that which is Christ's, more than enemies and foes: but He that is good still shows them kindness, and calls them to repentance.[73]

285. Glory be to thee, O Lord, glory be to thee! What an abyss of love to man is with thee! What wealth of long-suffering! They who, for thy own Name's sake, from being abject and unhonoured, become honoured and respected, have used their honour against him that has honoured them: they dare what should not be ventured upon, and outrage the things which are holy, thrusting out and rejecting those who are in earnest, in order that in great quiet and with absolute security, the wicked may subvert everything they choose.

286. And if you desire to learn the causes of so shocking an affair, you will find them to be like the former. For they have one root, and (so to speak) one mother, which is envy. They are not of one species however, but are different.

287. For it is said, 'Let one be rejected because he is young;' and another, 'Because he does not know how to flatter;' and another, 'Because he has affronted such a one;' and another, 'That such a one may not be grieved when he sees the one he has proposed, not accepted, and this one appointed;' and another, 'Because he is kind and devout;' and another, 'Because he is terrible to evil doers;' and another for some like reason: for they do not lack pretences, however many they want. Even the abundance of aspirants is alleged by them as a reason, when they have nothing else; and that a man ought not to be rashly promoted to this honour, but gradually and little by little: and they would be able to find as many other reasons as they might wish.

288. I may readily ask you here; What then ought the bishop to do who contends with such winds? How shall he withstand so many waves? How shall he repel all these assaults?

289. For if the matter is managed by right reason, all become enemies and hostile both to him (the bishop) and to those who are appointed; and they do everything with him contentiously, raising seditions daily, and heaping countless insults upon those who are appointed, until they either expel them, or bring in their own friends. And it happens almost as when a sea-captain has sailing with him in the ship pirates who constantly and every moment plot against him, the sailors, and the passengers.

290. And if he prefers their favour to his own salvation by receiving whom he ought not, he will have as his enemy God instead of them, than which what can be worse? And as for them, it will be more difficult for him than before; since they will co-operate with one another, and so become the stronger. For as when fierce opposing winds beat hard, the sea which before was calm, suddenly rages and foams,

---

71 Ezek. xxxiii. 11.

72 Ezek. xviii. 23, xxiii. 33.

73 Tit. iii. 4; Rom. ii. 4; 2 Pet. iii. 9.

and destroys those that sail upon it, so also the tranquillity of the Church, when she admits base men, is overspread with tempest and many wrecks.

XVI. WHAT SORT OF MAN HE MUST BE WHO HAS TO ENCOUNTER SO MANY STORMS.

291. Consider then, what he should be who has to encounter such a storm, that he may deal rightly with so many hindrances to the common welfare.

292. For he must be grave and without haughtiness, reverend and benign, commanding and communicable, impartial and courteous, humble and not servile, energetic and gentle, in order that he may be able to contend easily against all these things, and to introduce the proper man with much authority, even though all should oppose him; and with the same authority, not to bring in him that is unfit, even though all should consent, but to look to one thing alone,—the edification of the Church, and to do nothing through enmity or favour.

293. Do you not think I have done right in refusing the business of this ministry? and I have not yet gone through all to you, for I have other things to say. But be not weary of bearing with a man who is your genuine friend, and wishes to persuade you in reference to what you charge him with. For these things are not only advantageous to my defence before you, but will perhaps confer no small benefit towards the conduct of the office.

294. It is necessary that he who is about to enter upon this course of life, should before all things well examine everything, and so embrace the ministry. For what reason? If for no other, at least for this: that it is the good fortune of one who wisely understands all such things, not to be taken by surprise when they occur.

295. Do you wish then, that I should first treat of the oversight of widows, the care of virgins, or the difficulty of the judicial department? There is in each of these a different kind of solicitude, and a fear even greater than the solicitude.

296. And first, to make a beginning with what appears easier than the others—the oversight of widows; it seems indeed only to cause those who look after the funds, concern respecting their expenditure. But this is not the case; it also requires minute examination, when it is needful to enrol them.

297. Because, to enter their names rashly and as it happens, works innumerable mischiefs. For they (widows) have ruined houses, and dissolved marriages, and been often caught in thefts and frauds, and misbehaving themselves in other like manner.

298. Now that such should be supported by the funds of the Church, brings vengeance from God, and utter condemnation from men, and renders those who are willing to do good more slow to do it. Who could ever choose, that the money which Christ commanded to be given, should be squandered upon those who vilify the name of Christ?

299. Therefore the examination which is made must be extensive and severe, so that both such as have been mentioned, and such as are able to provide for themselves, should not defile the table of those who are helpless.

300. And after this examination, another no small care succeeds;—that the supply of provision may flow in upon them freely, as if from fountains, and never fail.

For somehow involuntary poverty is an insatiable evil, and complaining, and ungrateful; and there is need of much prudence, and of much diligence, to stop their mouths and to take away all pretext for finding fault.

301. Many, when they see one who is superior to avarice, forthwith fancy him to be fitted for this ministration; but I think this largeness of heart is not alone sufficient, though it is needed before other virtues (for without this a man would rather be a destroyer than a manager, a wolf instead of a shepherd), and that with it we should ask whether he happens to possess another: I refer to patience, the cause of all good things to men; which brings and conveys the soul as it were into some peaceful haven.

302. The class of widows, on account of poverty, age, and sex, employ immeasurable freedom of speech (for so it is better to call it), and they cry out unseasonably, and find fault without cause, and murmur over what they ought to be thankful for, and complain about what ought to be approved of. Yet he that has the oversight must bear all generously, and be provoked neither by their unseasonable annoyances, nor by their unreasonable repinings.

303. It is right that the class should be pitied, and not reproached for their misfortunes; so that to insult over their calamities, and to add to the pain caused by poverty, that arising from contempt, would be the extreme of cruelty.

304. Therefore, one of the wisest men, contemplating the avarice and disdainfulness of the human race, and observing the nature of poverty that it is fearful, and prostrates the most generous soul, and often causes it to be without shame in regard to such things; (that he who is entreated by them might not be offended, nor he who ought to aid them, become their enemy when provoked by the constancy of their supplications,) advises us to be gentle and accessible to the needy, saying, "Incline thine ear to the poor without grief, and answer him peaceably in meekness."[74] And putting aside him that annoys (for what can one say to the fallen?) he converses with him that can bear another's infirmity, urging him to lift him up, by kindness of looks, and by gentleness of speech, before the gift is bestowed.

305. Now even if one should not take from what is theirs, but yet should cover them with reproaches, and insult them and be angry with them, not only would he fail to relieve the sadness of poverty by giving, but he would make the evil greater by his chiding.

306. For although they are driven by bodily necessity to be very unabashed, they are nevertheless grieved by this violence. Since then, they are forced to beg through fear of want, and become insolent through begging, and through being insolent again are despised, what I may call a multiform power of sadness, which brings great gloom, overshadows their soul.

307. He who has the care of them ought to be so long-suffering as not only not to increase their sorrow by his own indignation, but to mitigate the more by his consolation that which they experience. For as when one in great abundance is reproached, he does not realise the benefit of his wealth because he is wounded by the reproach; so he who hears a kind word, and receives a gift, and comfort as well, rejoices and is glad, and so his gift is doubled.

---

74 Ecclus. iv. 8.

308. I say not this of myself, but after him who before exhorted us; for he says, "My son, in doing good administer no rebuke, nor grievous speech with any gift. Will not the dew assuage heat? So a word is better than a gift. For behold, a word is better than a gift, and both are with a gracious man."[75]

309. He who superintends these things, must not only be gentle and long-suffering, but none the less able to manage; for if this be lacking, the goods of the poor are involved in just as much mischief.

310. Some time ago, one who had been entrusted with this service, collected a large amount of money which he did not swallow up himself; neither did he expend it on the needy, with the exception of a few; but he dug a hole to keep most of it in, until a time of danger arose, and then he betrayed it into the hands of enemies.

311. There must therefore be great precaution, that the property of the Church may neither be superfluous nor fail; but all that has been contributed is to be quickly dispersed among the poor, and the treasures of the Church are to be accumulated in the predilections of its subordinate members.

312. In the entertaining of strangers, and helping the sick, how much expenditure of money, think you, is required! What accuracy and wisdom in those who have the superintendence! for this (casual) expenditure is by no means less than the one before named, but often is necessarily greater; and he who superintends must be one who is able to give with respect and prudence; that he may induce those who are in possession of wealth to bestow it zealously and joyously, and that he way not wound the feelings of contributors while providing for the refreshment of the sick.

313. Much greater patience and diligence ought to be manifested here; for somehow the sick are hard to please, and dull, and unless exactness and care be applied every way, any small matter overlooked suffices to cause great mischief to a sick man.

XVII. GREAT CAUTION DEMANDED BY THE SPIRITUAL OVERSIGHT OF VIRGINS.

314. With reference to the care of the virgins, the apprehension is all the greater, in that this group is a more honourable and princely possession than the others. Even into the circle of these holy ones, multitudes full of innumerable evils have intruded themselves. Here then the trouble is greater.

315. And as it is not the same thing for a maiden who is free, and for her serving woman to sin, so not for a virgin and a widow; because it has become a matter of indifference for widows to talk foolishly, and to revile one another, and to flatter, and to be shameless, and to appear everywhere, and to parade in the public places; but the virgin has prepared herself for greater things, and entered on the pursuit of the wisdom which is above, and professed to exhibit upon earth the conduct of the angels; and while she is in this body it is her purpose to display the qualities of incorporeal powers; and she neither ought to take many and superfluous walks, nor is allowed to utter words idly and in vain, and it behoves her not even to know the name of reviling and flattery.

316. On this account she needs the safest protection and a greater defence. For

---

75 Ecclus. xviii. 15–17.

the enemy of holiness constantly and especially attends upon such, and lies in wait, ready to devour, any one who may happen to stumble and fall; and there are many men who plot against them; and with all these things there is the madness of nature; so that they have to make preparation against a twofold war, — the one which assails them from without, and that which troubles them within.

317. Therefore he who has the care of them has great fear, and greater danger and anguish if anything unforeseen should ever occur, — which God forbid.

318. For if "a daughter in privacy is a cause of wakefulness to her father, and care about her takes away sleep;"[76] where there is so much fear about her being childless, or passing the flower of youth unmarried, or being disliked, — what shall he do who is solicitous, not about any of these things, but others far greater than they? For here it is not a man who repudiates, but Christ himself; nor does sterility only extend to reproaches, but the mischief terminates in the ruin of the soul; for, says He, "Every tree which produceth not good fruit is hewn down, and cast into the fire;"[77] nor is it enough for her who is hated by the Bridegroom to take a bill of divorcement and to go away;[78] but she pays the penalty of that hatred, — eternal punishment.[79]

319. He who is a father after the flesh, has many things which make the custody of a daughter easy; because a mother, and a nurse, and a crowd of serving women, and the safety of a house, co-operate with the father in the keeping of the virgin. She is not allowed frequently to enter public places; nor, when she enters them, is she forced to be seen by any who meet her, since the dusk of evening no less than the walls of a house, may conceal her who would not be seen.

320. But without these things, she is free from all blame, so long as she is not forced to come into the presence of men. For neither care for necessaries, nor the insults of those who wrong her, nor anything else of that sort, imposes upon her the necessity for such an occurrence, because her father is to her in the place of every body; but she has one concern only — neither to say nor to do anything unworthy of the decorum which befits her.

321. But in our case there are many things which render such guardianship difficult, or rather impossible to the father; for he could not have her at home with him, since such residence together would neither be becoming, nor free from danger. And even if they did no wrong but persevered in preserving their sanctity unsullied, they would render no less account for the souls which they had caused to stumble than if they had sinned against each other. Since then this is impossible, neither is it practicable to ascertain the movements of her mind, to cut off such of them as are irregularly disposed, and to train and conduct to what is better, such as are orderly and harmonious. Nor is it easy to pry into her walks abroad.

---

76 Ecclus. xlii. 9. Another reading of this passage is represented by the English version: "The father waketh for the daughter when no man knoweth; and the care for her taketh away sleep."

77 Matt. iii. 10; vii. 19.

78 Deut. xxiv. 1; Mark x. 4.

79 Matt. xxv. 46.

322. Poverty and want of protection do not allow him to search narrowly into what ought to be her behaviour. When she is forced to manage her own affairs she has many pretexts for going abroad, if she is not inclined to be prudent; and he who bids her always stop at home, and cut off the occasions for it, is bound to provide her with a sufficiency of necessaries, and a female to serve her in such things, and he must prevent her from going to funerals and night vigils; for that most crafty serpent knows how to scatter his venom even by means of good deeds. A virgin ought to be fenced in on all sides, and to leave her house very seldom in the course of the year, and only when unavoidable and necessary causes compel her.

323. If any one should say there is no need for a bishop to occupy himself with such things, know well, that anxieties and accusations which concern every one, are referred to him; and it is far better that by managing everything he should be freed from blame which he must bear for the sins of others, than that by avoiding such management, he should be in fear of investigations arising out of what others have done.

324. And besides, he who does these things himself, very easily passes through everything; but he who is compelled to do this while persuading the minds of others, has less respite from remitting his own labour, than toil and trouble from those who oppose and contend against his decisions.

325. But I could not enumerate all the anxieties which arise on account of virgins, for even when they have to be registered they give no ordinary occupation to him that is entrusted with this ministration.

XVIII. THE OFFICE OF JUDGE A DIFFICULT ONE.

326. As for the judicial part, it involves innumerable difficulties, much toil, and more perplexities than even those endure who sit in judgment in civil cases. It is both a task to find out what is right, and hard not to go wrong when one has found it.

327. Not only is there toil and perplexity, but no small danger; for already some of our weaker friends who have become involved in such matters, have made shipwreck of faith because they have had none to patronize them.

328. For many who have suffered wrong, no less than those who have done wrong, hate them that do not help them, and will not take into account either the distraction of business, or the difficulty of the occasion, or the mediocrity of priestly power, or any such thing; but they are unforgiving judges who know of only one plea, — deliverance from the evils which oppress them. He who cannot grant them this, even though he urge ten thousand excuses, will never escape from their condemnation.

329. But since I have mentioned patronage, let me discover to you another pretext for blame. For unless he who is a bishop makes daily visits to houses more often than a lounger would, unspeakable offences arise from it. For not only the sick but those in health wish to be looked after, not because their piety prompts them to this, but most of them because they affect honour and dignity. If he ever happens to seem more attentive to the more wealthy and powerful, though necessity compels it for the common good of the Church, he straightway acquires a reputation for

flattery and adulation.

330. But why do I speak of patronage and visitings? From his very greetings alone, they derive such a load of accusations, that he is burdened and often falls under his despondency. Nay, they actually subject his very look to investigation. Many strictly test what he does unconsciously, making inquiry into the tone of his voice, the expression of his countenance, and the extent to which he smiles and laughs. 'Upon such a one,' say they, 'he smiled most graciously, and addressed him with a beaming face and a loud voice, but we got less even than usual.' And if many sit together, and he does not cast his eyes all round when he speaks, others say a slight is put upon them.

331. Who then that is not very strong is able to contend with such accusers? or to avoid being accused? or to escape when he is accused? He ought indeed to have no accusers; but if this be impossible, he ought to be absolved from their accusations. And if this also is impracticable, but some will take pleasure in accusing idly and without cause, he must nobly bear up against the sorrow arising from such rebukes.

332. He that is justly accused, may easily bear with his accuser, because there is no sterner accuser than conscience; therefore, when we are overtaken by the severest of all, we easily endure external accusers as more gentle. But he who is not conscious of having a fault, when he is accused without cause, is quickly borne away by anger, and easily falls into despondency, unless he has prepared himself beforehand to bear the follies of the many. It is by no means possible that one who is maligned and condemned for nothing, should not be disturbed, and somewhat pained by such unreasonableness.

333. Who can tell what grief they endure when it is necessary to cut one off from the community of the Church?

334. Would indeed that the mischief consisted only in grief! but there is no small loss as well. There is the fear lest being chastised beyond what is fitting, he should suffer what is spoken of by the blessed Paul:—"and be swallowed up with overmuch sorrow."[80]

335. Therefore there is here also need of extreme exactness, lest the intention to profit, should become to him the occasion of greater loss.

336. For whatever sins he commits after such a remedy is resorted to, the physician who does not rightly treat the wound, will partake in the wrath incurred by each of them.

337. What vengeance then must he expect, who must not only render an account of the transgressions he himself commits, but is exposed to utmost peril for sins committed by others? For if we are afraid to suffer investigation of our proper trespasses, because unable to escape the fire, what should he expect to suffer who shall answer for so many?

338. For that this is true, hear the blessed Paul saying, or rather not him, but Christ speaking in him: "Obey them that have the rule over you, and submit, for they watch for your souls, as they that must render an account."[81]

---

80 2 Cor. ii. 7.

81 Heb. xiii. 17.

339. Is the terror of this threatening small? It cannot be told.

340. All these things however, are enough to persuade even those who are very unbelieving and stubborn, that I made my escape, not because I was affected by pride and vain-glory, but only because I feared for myself, and had regard to the weightiness of the obligation.

Book IV.

I. Not only those who are anxious to enter the clerical office are severely corrected for the sins they commit, but those also who are constrained to accept it.

341. When Basil had heard these things and paused a little, he said:

[BASIL.] Well, if you had been anxious to obtain possession of this dignity, this your fear would have been reasonable.

342. For he who by his anxiety to receive it has avowed himself qualified for the discharge of the function, is not permitted, after being entrusted with it, to shelter himself under his inexperience, when he fails in any respect; for he has already deprived himself of this line of defence, by rushing forward and seizing the ministry; and the man who comes to it willingly and voluntarily cannot say, "I committed such a sin involuntarily, and involuntarily did such and such mischief."

343. For he who pronounces judgment on him in this matter, will say, "And why, when you were self-conscious of such inexperience, and of not having talent equal to the faultless execution of this task, were you so eager and venturesome as to undertake duties which were beyond your proper ability? who compelled you? who forcibly drew you when reluctant and averse?"

344. But you would never hear anything of this kind. Nor could you bring any such accusation against yourself. And it is manifest to all, that you had no desire, whether small or great, for this honour; but it was the determination of others; and that which permits them to have no absolution for their faults, furnishes you with a good ground of defence.

345. I nodded assent to this, and quietly smiled, admiring his simplicity, and said:

[CHRYSOSTOM.] I have also myself wished the matter might be as you say, my most excellent friend; not that I might obtain what I have now avoided. For even if no punishment awaited me, as one who without skill took charge of the flock of Christ, still it would be more painful to me than any punishment, that when concerns so great had been committed to me I should seem so base towards him that entrusted me with them.

346. Why then should I desire that opinion of yours not to be wrong? That those wretched and miserable men,—for so I am bound to call such as are incapable of properly filling this office, even though you should say a thousand times that they were brought in by force, and sinned ignorantly,—that they may escape the unquenchable fire, and the outer darkness, and the worm which dieth not, and the

cutting asunder, and perdition along with the hypocrites.[82] But why do I trouble you? It is assuredly not so.

347. And if you will, I will offer you the proof of what I have said; first from a kingdom, which is not of so great account with God as the priesthood is.

348. Saul, the son of Kish, was made a king when he was not deserving it, but had gone forth to seek after the asses, and had begun to ask the prophet about them; and he spoke to him of the kingdom. Nor even then did he press forward, although he heard it from a man who was a prophet; but he shrunk from it, and refused it, saying:—"Who am I, and what is my father's house?"[83] What then? When he had misemployed the honour which God gave him, could these words of his deliver him from the anger of Him that had made him king?

349. Yet he might have said to Samuel when he rebuked him, "Did I invade the kingly office? Did I rush into this authority? I wished to lead the easy and quiet life of private persons, but you dragged me to this dignity. If I had remained in my humble position, I should have easily avoided these offences. Nor indeed, if I had been one of the multitude, and without distinction, should I have been appointed to this task, neither would God have committed to me the war against the Amalekites; and if I had not been entrusted with it, I should not have committed this sin."

350. But all this is powerless as a defence, and not only powerless, but perilous, and inflames God's anger the more.[84]

351. For he that is honoured beyond his desert, ought not to urge the greatness of his honour as an apology for his sins, but to employ God's great regard for him as a motive to greater excellence.

352. But he that supposes that he is allowed to sin because he has attained to greater dignity, is anxious for nothing else than to prove the love of God the cause of his personal offences. To say this is always the habit of the wicked and such as lead a careless life. But we ought not to be thus disposed, nor to fall into like madness with them, but to be every way anxious to employ what we have to the best of our ability, and to control both our tongue and our thoughts.

353. And now, leaving the kingdom, let us come to the priesthood, which is the matter in hand. Eli was not anxious to acquire this honour; but what profit was this to him when he sinned? And why do I say 'to acquire' it? He could not have avoided it if he would, for the law compelled him; for he was of the tribe of Levi, and was bound to accept the office which descended to him from his fathers. Yet even he suffered no slight punishment through the profligacy of his sons.[85]

354. He also who was the first priest of the Jews, of whom God spake so much to Moses; when he was unable alone to resist the madness of so great a multitude, was he not very nearly destroyed, although the intercession of his brother turned

---

82 Mark ix. 43–48; Matt. viii. 12; xxiv. 51.

83 2 Sam. 9.

84 1 Sam. 15.

85 1 Sam. ii. 22–36; iv. 18.

away the wrath of God?[86]

355. And since I have mentioned Moses, it will be as well to show the truth of my argument from his experience. For the blessed Moses was so far from seizing the leadership of the Jews, that he declined it when offered him, and refused it when God commanded, and to such an extent as to provoke Him that appointed him.[87] And not then alone, but even afterwards, when he had entered upon his office, he would have willingly died to be exempt from it; for he says, "Kill me, if thou art about to deal thus with me."[88]

356. What then? When he had sinned in regard to the water (of Meribah), did his continual deprecations avail to make excuse for him, and to persuade God to vouchsafe him remission?[89] For what other reason was he deprived of the promised land? For no other whatever, as we all know, than for this sin, through which that wonderful man was unable to attain the same as those who were subject to him; but after many toils and miseries, after that indescribable wandering, and his wars and trophies, he died out of the land for which he had suffered so much; and after he had borne the dangers of the sea, he did not enjoy the benefit of the haven.

357. Do you see that neither to those who seize office, nor to those who attain it through the zeal of others, does there remain any excuse for the sins they commit? For if they who often refused, though God appointed, suffered so much punishment, and nothing availed to deliver from this danger either Aaron or Eli, or that blessed man, the saint, the prophet, the wonderful man who was more meek than any upon earth, with whom God talked as with a friend, it will scarcely be a sufficient apology for us, who are not endowed with his virtue, that we are conscious of having been in no wise anxious for this office, and especially since many of these ordinations do not originate in the grace of God, but the forwardness of men.

358. God elected Judas, and enrolled him with that holy company, and ordained him to the apostolic dignity along with the rest; and even gave him something more than the others, the management of the funds. What then? When he had abused both these things, and betrayed Him whom he was commissioned to preach, and basely squandered what he had been ordained to dispense, did he escape from punishment? For this very cause he brought upon himself severer vengeance. And very properly.

359. For we ought not to offend God by misusing the honours which God has given; but to please Him the more.

360. But he who has received the greater honour, and desires on this account to go scot-free where he ought to suffer chastisement, does much the same as if one of the unbelieving Jews on hearing Christ say, "If I had not come and spoken to them, they would not have had sin;"[90] and, "If I had not done the miracles among them

---

86 Ex. xxxii. 10.

87 Ex. iv. 10–16.

88 Num. xi. 15.

89 Num. xx. 12, 13.

90 John xv. 22.

which no one else did, they would not have had sin,"[91] had accused his Saviour and Benefactor by saying, "Then why didst thou come and speak? Why didst thou work miracles, in order to punish us the more?"

361. But these are the words of madness and utter insanity. For the Physician came not that you might be the rather condemned; He came to heal, yea, to deliver you perfectly from your disease. But you have voluntarily taken yourself out of his hands, therefore receive severer punishment. For as you would have been freed from your former guilt if you had yielded to the remedy, so because you have avoided Him when you saw Him present, you will no longer be able to purge it away; and not being able, you will be punished for it, and that because you have, on your part, rendered all his solicitude ineffectual.

362. Therefore we are not subject to the same test before we receive honour from God, as we are after the honour is given, but the latter is by far the severer. For he who is not made good by kindness, would be justly punished more sharply.

363. Because then, this defence is shown to be weak, and will not only not deliver those who take refuge in it, but exposes them the more, we must provide ourselves with other security.

[BASIL.] 364. And what is that? For I am unable now to retain my self-possession, you have made me so fearful and trembling by what you have said.

[CHRYSOSTOM.] 365. I pray and beseech you, said I, do not be so dejected. For there is most assuredly security for us that are feeble—never to become involved; and for you that are strong—to rest your hopes of salvation in nought, after God's grace, except the doing of nothing unworthy of this gift and of God who has given it.

366. They would be deserving of the greatest chastisement, who, after acquiring this dignity by personal exertion, discharge its functions amiss, either because of their negligence, or wickedness, or even of their unskilfulness. Nor is there left any indulgence on this ground to such as have not been anxious for the office; but these too will be deprived of all excuse.

367. For I think, that even if myriads should invite and urge, they ought not to be regarded; but that after having first put his own soul to the test, and made minute inspection of everything, then one should yield to those who constrain him.

368. And now, no man who is not a builder, would venture to promise to build a house; nor would anybody undertake to prescribe for the sick if he knew nothing of medical practice; but although many should forcibly urge him, such a one would refuse, and not blush over his ignorance. And shall not he first examine himself who is about to be entrusted with the care of so many souls? If he be wholly unqualified, shall he accept the office because such a one bids him, or such a one forces him, or not to offend so and so?

369. Will he not hurl himself along with them into evident harm? When he could have saved himself by keeping to himself, he draws others into ruin as well as himself. Whence can we hope for salvation? Whence can we procure forgiveness? Who will then plead for us? Will they perchance, who now compel us and drag us into this necessity? But who will then deliver them? For they also need the aid of

---

91 John xv. 24.

others that they may escape the fire.

370. But that you may know I do not say these things now to terrify you, but as truth demands, hear what the blessed Paul says to Timothy his own and beloved son: "Lay hands suddenly on no man, nor be a partaker in other men's sins."[92]

371. Do you see now from what blame and chastisement, I, for my part, have delivered those who were going to lead me into this position?

II. SUCH AS ORDAIN THE UNWORTHY WILL SUFFER THE SAME PUNISHMENT, EVEN IF THEY ARE UNACQUAINTED WITH THOSE WHO ARE ORDAINED.

372. It is not enough for their defence, that such as have been elected should say, "I did not come forward of my own choice; and I did not withdraw because I did not foreknow the event." And in like manner, what gain could it be to those who confer ordination, if they should say they were unacquainted with him that was ordained?

373. On this very account their blame is greater because they have promoted him they knew not, and what they fancy to be an apology, will increase their condemnation.

374. For is it not inconsistent, that when they wish to buy a slave, they show him to doctors, and require sureties for the purchase, and make inquiry of the neighbours, and have no confidence after all this, but ask for a long time to make trial of him; and yet, when if they are about to designate any one to so great a ministry, they come to a decision heedlessly and by chance, if it pleases somebody to give a certificate through partiality or enmity towards others, and make no further inquiry?

375. Who will then plead for us, when they who ought to be our advocates, themselves need intercessors?

376. Wherefore, he that is intending to confer ordination, must make diligent investigation; and much more he that is to be ordained.

377. For although this one has as partakers of chastisement for his sins, those who appointed him, he will not be relieved from punishment himself, but will suffer even more than they.

378. Provided only that they who elected him did not, from some human motive, act contrary to what seemed to them right. For if they were detected in this, and through some pretext advanced one whom they knew to be unworthy, equal punishments, and perhaps even greater, would be awarded to such as appointed the unsuitable person. For he that gives authority to one who is ready to injure the church, would be guilty of such a man's rash deeds.

379. And if he were responsible for none of these things, and should say he was deceived by the judgment of the majority, not even then would he remain exculpated, but would suffer less punishment than the one who was ordained. Why so? Because it is probable that those who made the election, decided upon it through being deceived by an opinion which was false; but he that had been elected could no longer say, 'I did not know myself,' as the others could. As therefore he will be punished more severely than those who brought him forward, so must he make a

---

92 1 Tim. v. 22.

more severe examination of himself than they: and if they should introduce him ignorantly, he must be prompt to teach them the reasons by which he may stay those who are deceived, and by showing himself to be unworthy of trial, escape the burden of so great a task.

380. Why is it that in war, and trade, and agriculture, and other worldly affairs, counsel is taken beforehand, and the husbandman does not choose to navigate a ship, nor the soldier to cultivate the ground, nor a sailor to make war, though one should threaten them with a thousand deaths? Manifestly because each of them foresees the peril of incompetency.

381. If then, where there is danger in small affairs, we shall employ so much forethought, and will not yield to the constraint of such as force us; shall we, where eternal punishment awaits those who ignorantly fill the priestly office, expose ourselves rashly and inconsiderately to so great a peril, alleging that we are compelled by others? He will not tolerate it, who shall then judge us for this.

382. Far greater precaution must be displayed about spiritual than about temporal matters; but we are not found now to exhibit so much.

383. For tell me, if, supposing a man to be an artificer who was not an artificer, we summoned him to work, and he obeyed, but after taking in hand the materials prepared for a house, he spoiled the wood, and spoiled the stones, and should construct the house so that it fell to ruin at once; would it suffice for his defence that he was induced by others, and did not come of his own election? By no means; and very properly and justly so, for he ought to have resisted, though others invited him.

384. If then there is no escape from punishment to him who ruins wood and stone; shall he who destroys souls and carelessly builds them up, think that the necessity imposed on him by others is sufficient for his deliverance?

385. Would not this be very foolish? For I have not yet added, that no one will be able to compel him that will not. But so be it, that he has been exposed to all sorts of violence, and stratagems of every kind, so that he succumbs; will this deliver him from punishment? Let us not, I pray, so deceive ourselves, nor feign that we are ignorant of what is evident to very children. For the pretext of ignorance will not profit us when we are called to an account.

386. You have not been anxious to receive this office, because you were conscious of your weakness? Well and good. Therefore, with this disposition, you ought to have resisted when others invited. When no one invited you, were you weak and unfitted; but when men were found ready to bestow the honour, did you suddenly become able?

387. Such things are ridiculous and vain, and worthy of extreme punishment. Therefore also our Lord exhorts him who means to build a tower, not to lay the foundation before he calculates his personal ability, that he may not afford to such as pass by abundant occasion to mock at him.[93] The injury to him extends only to ridicule. But here the punishment is fire unquenchable, and an undying worm, and gnashing of teeth, and outer darkness, and cutting asunder, and a place among the

---

93 Luke xiv. 28.

hypocrites.[94]

388. But my accusers will look at none of these things, or they would have ceased to blame one that was unwilling to destroy himself without cause.

389. The supervision which is proposed to us, is not that of wheat or barley, nor of oxen and sheep, nor of other like matters, but of the very body of Jesus.

390. For the Church of Christ, according to the blessed Paul, is the body of Christ,[95] and he who has had this confided to him ought to train it to great healthfulness and inimitable loveliness, watching on every side that there may be neither spot nor wrinkle, nor any other like stain to blemish its beauty and comeliness; and what else, save that to the extent of human power, he may make it appear worthy of that immortal and blessed Head which it possesses?

391. For if they who aspire to athletic vigour have need of physicians, and trainers, and careful diet, and constant exercise, and countless attentions besides,—because when anything is casually overlooked, it subverts and frustrates the whole,—how shall they whose lot it is to minister to this body (the Church), which has to contend not against men but against invisible powers, be able to preserve it in purity and health, unless they can transcend human virtue, and understand every remedy which befits the soul?

III. GREAT ABILITY TO SPEAK IS REQUIRED OF A PRIEST.

392. Know you not that this body (the Church) is subject to even more diseases and attacks than our body of flesh, becomes more rapidly corrupt, and is more slowly healed?

393. For they who heal men's bodies have invented divers remedies, a varied apparatus of instruments, and diet adapted to the sick; while the condition of the atmosphere alone is often sufficient for the restoration of an invalid; and there are cases in which an opportune falling asleep has freed the physician from all trouble.

394. But here, none of these things are to be thought of. After works (or example) there is vouchsafed but one plan and method of cure,—verbal instruction: this is the instrument, this is the diet, this is the most genial climate: this stands for physic, for cautery, and for the knife. If there must be cautery and incision, one must perforce use this. If this avail not, everything else goes for nothing. By this we arouse the dejected soul, and reduce the inflamed, and amputate excrescences, and supply defects, and do all that contributes to the health of the soul.

395. The life of another man may indeed produce an equal zeal for the best regulation of life; but when the soul is sick through spurious doctrines, there is in this case much need of discourse, not only for security at home, but against external conflicts.

396. For if any one should have such a sword of the Spirit and shield of faith that he could work wonders, and by miracles stop the mouths of the shameless,[96] he would require no help from discourse; or rather not even then would it be useless,

---

94 Is. lxvi. 24; Matt. iii. 12; Matt. xxiv. 51; xxv. 31; Mark ix. 43.

95 Col. i. 18; Eph. v. 23, 30.

96 1 Cor. xiii. 2; Eph. vi. 17; Tit. i. 11; Heb. xi. 33.

but even very needful.

397. For the blessed Paul also employed it, although wondered at everywhere for his miracles. And another of the same company, exhorts us to be mindful of this influence; saying: "Be ready to give an answer to every man who asks you a reason for the hope that is in you."[97] And all together at that time entrusted to those who accompanied Stephen, the management of the widows, for no other reason, than that they themselves might have leisure for the ministry of the word.[98]

398. Nevertheless, we should not so greatly require it, if we had the power of miracles. But if no trace of this power remains, and many enemies constantly assail us on every side, it remains that we must fortify ourselves with this, that we may not be smitten by the arrows of the enemies, and that we may smite them.

399. Wherefore we must be greatly concerned, that the word of Christ may dwell in us richly.[99]

IV. THE PRIEST SHOULD BE PREPARED TO CONTEND WITH GREEKS (PAGANS), JEWS, AND HERETICS.

Our equipment is not for one kind of battle only, but this war is diversified, and carried on by various enemies. They do not employ the same weapons, nor are they concerned to attack us in the same manner.

400. He that is going to enter into battle with them all, must know the tactics of them all, and the same man must be archer and slinger, centurion and commander of a cohort, private soldier and general, footman and horseman, marine, and artilleryman.

401. In military engagements every man undertakes one duty in the performance of which he repels assailants. But it is not so here; and if he who is to conquer understands not all the forms of military art, the devil knows how to plunder the sheep by leading in his bandits through the one place which may be overlooked; but not when he perceives a shepherd to be coming who has perfect knowledge, and well understands his devices.

402. Therefore we must be well defended on all sides. A city, so long as it is fortified all round, mocks at besiegers, and continues in great security; but if any one should break down the wall only the width of a doorway, no advantage remains to it from the surrounding fence, although all the remainder stands firm. So is also the city of God. When the promptitude and understanding of the pastor surround it on every side like a wall, all stratagems end in shame and derision to the enemies, and those who dwell within abide secure; but when any succeeds in demolishing it in part, even though he do not break down the whole, I may say that by means of a portion all that remains is ruined. For what if one successfully contended against the Greeks, but the Jews despoiled him? or should conquer both, but the Manichæans plundered him? or if, after getting the better of these, those who bring in

---

97 1 Pet. iii. 15.

98 Acts vi. 4.

99 Col. iii. 16.

fatalism should slay the sheep which are within? But why must I enumerate all the devil's heresies? If the pastor does not well understand how to repel them all, the wolf by means of one of them may be able to devour most of the sheep.

403. In the case of soldiers, again, it is always to be expected that victory and slaughter will come from those who stand and fight; but here it is very different; for conflict with others has frequently conferred the triumph upon those who have been sitting at ease, and have not fought from the outset, nor have toiled at all; and he who is wounded by his own sword because he has not much skill in such matters, becomes ridiculous both to friends and foes.

404. I will try to make what I say clear to you by an example. They who have adopted the foolish opinion of Valentinus and Marcion, and all that are similarly insane, reject from the catalogue of the divine writings the law which was given by God to Moses. But the Jews honour it so much that even though the times forbid, they contend in opposition to God's intention, for its complete observance. Now the Church of God, avoiding the exaggeration of both, pursues the middle course, and neither urges submission to its yoke, nor allows us to malign it, but commends that which has been annulled, because it was once useful in its time.

405. He who is to contend with both, must understand this proportion and mean; for if he would teach the Jews that their adhesion to the old law is out of date, and should begin by accusing it unsparingly, he would afford no slight handle to such of the heretics as wish to traduce it; but if he should be anxious to stop their mouths, and immoderately exalt it, and admire it as actually necessary at the present time, he would open the mouth of the Jews.

406. They again who rage with the madness of Sabellius, and rave after the manner of Arius, have fallen from the sound faith through going to extremes. The name of Christians is indeed applied to both, but if any one should test their doctrine, he would find the one party no better than the Jews, save in so far as they differ in names; the other party to have great affinity to the heresy of Paul of Samosata; and both to be far from the truth.

407. There is therefore, much danger here too; the road is narrow and strait, and shut in by precipices on both sides; and there is no little apprehension lest he who would smite another should be struck by a third. If we say the Godhead is one, Sabellius forthwith perverts the expression in favour of his own folly; and if again a distinction is made by saying the Father is one, and the Son another, and the Holy Ghost another, Arius comes in perverting the distinction of Persons into a difference of substance. But we must turn aside and flee from both the impious confusion of the one, and the insane division of the other, confessing the one Godhead of the Father, Son, and Holy Ghost, and adding the three Persons; for so shall we be able to repel the invasions of both.

408. I could tell you of many other engagements from which, if a man fight not against them nobly, and carefully, he departs with many wounds.

V. THE PRIEST OUGHT TO BE WELL SKILLED IN THE ART OF REASONING.

409. Why should one mention the carpings of private persons? For these are not

less than external assaults, and even afford more toil and trouble to a teacher. Some, through meddlesomeness, without cause and to no purpose, wish to interfere in what cannot be learned, and would not profit them if they could learn it. Others again, require of him investigations into the judgments of God, and force him to fathom the great abyss: for, (says the Psalmist), 'Thy judgments are a great deep.'[100]

410. As for faith and personal behaviour, you will find few that are anxious about them; but many more who busy themselves and ask questions about things which it is not possible to explore, and the search after which provokes God. For when we strive to learn what He wills we should not know, we shall never know it. (How can we if God is unwilling?) And the only result is to run into danger through our inquisitiveness.

411. Nevertheless, although such is the case, if anyone should with authority silence those who search out these inexplicable matters, he wins for himself the reputation of folly and ignorance. Wherefore, he who is in office, must here employ great prudence, that he may divert them from improper inquiries, and avoid the accusations which have been mentioned.

412. Against all these things, no other help has been given than that of speech alone, and if anyone be destitute of that power, the souls of the men who are placed under him will be continually no better off than ships which are tempest-tossed; I mean those of the weaker and more inquisitive. Therefore the priest must do everything he can to acquire this faculty.

VI. Evidence supplied by S. Paul.

[BASIL.] 413. Why then, said he, was Paul not anxious to excel in this talent? He is not ashamed of his poverty of speech, but openly confesses that he is without skill; and this he addresses to the Corinthians, who were admired for their eloquence, and had high thoughts concerning it.[101]

[CHRYSOSTOM.] 414. It is this very thing, said I, which has ruined many, and has rendered them more careless about true doctrine. For being unable accurately to explore the depth of the minds of the Apostles, and to understand the purport of their words, they have passed their whole time in slumbering and yawning; and they have honoured, not the ignorance with which Paul said he was unlearned, but that which he was farther from than any other man under heaven.

415. But let this subject be deferred for a time; and meanwhile I say this: Let us suppose him to have been without skill in this respect, as they will, what is that to men at the present time?

416. He had a power far greater than that of speech, and one which could accomplish more. For only by making his appearance, and that in silence, he was terrible to demons; but if all the men of our day were to come together with countless prayers and tears, they could not do what the aprons from Paul once effected.[102]

417. Paul, by praying, raised the dead, and wrought other like miracles, so that

---

100 Ps. xxxvi. 6.

101 2 Cor. xi. 6.

102 Acts xix. 12.

he was even thought by the strangers to be a god.[103] And before he was removed from this life, he was counted worthy to be caught up to the third heaven, and to receive words which it is not lawful for human nature to hear.[104] But the men of our time, (I would not say anything harsh or offensive, and I say not these things now as blaming them, but because I am surprised,) somehow do not shudder to compare themselves with such a man.

418. For if, leaving out the miracles, we come to the life of that blessed man, and investigate his angelic conduct, you will see that the champion for Christ surpasses in this even more than in miracles. Why should we mention his zeal, his meekness, his constant perils, his thronging cares, his incessant griefs for the churches, his compassion for the rich, his many tribulations, his daily deaths?[105] What place in the world, what continent, what sea, knew not the conflicts of that righteous man? Even the uninhabited land knew him, and often received him when in danger. He endured every form of assault, and attained every kind of victory. He never ceased either to struggle or to triumph.

419. I know not how I have been induced to vilify that man; for his good deeds surpass all description, mine at any rate, as far as skilful orators surpass me. Nevertheless, not even for this reason will I desist, (for the saint will judge not by the result, but by the motive,) until I have said what exceeds all I have said, as much as he excels all men.

420. What then, is that? After so many good deeds, after innumerable laurels, he desired to go to Gehenna, and to be delivered to eternal punishment, in order that the Jews, who had often stoned him, and had slain him as far as they could, might be saved and come to Christ.[106] Who had such affection for Christ, if this ought to be called affection, and not rather something else, more than affection?

421. Shall we then, still compare ourselves with him, after so great grace as he received from above, and after so great virtue as he displayed in private? What would be more presumptuous than this?

422. Nor was he so unskilful in speech, as some think; and this, in fine, I shall try to prove.

423. They not only call him unskilled who is not practised in the arts of secular discourses, but also him who knows not how to contend for the doctrines of truth: and they are right in their opinion. Now, Paul did not say he was unskilled in both, but only in one; and in confirming this, he made a nice distinction, saying that he was unskilled in speech, but not in knowledge.

424. Now, if I required the polish of Isocrates, and the gravity of Demosthenes, the dignity of Thucydides, and the sublimity of Plato, I ought to bring forward this testimony of Paul. But I now dismiss all these, and the laboured embellishment of others, and do not concern myself with diction and enunciation. But let a man be impoverished in style, and simple and lax in the composition of words, only let him

---

103 Acts xiv. 11.

104 2 Cor. xii. 2.

105 2 Cor. xi. 23–29.

106 Rom. ix. 3.

not be unskilled in knowledge and accuracy of doctrine; nor let him, to conceal his personal negligence, take away from the saint the greatest of his excellences and the chief of his commendations.

VII. S. PAUL WAS ILLUSTRIOUS, NOT FOR HIS MIRACLES ONLY, BUT FOR HIS ELOQUENCE.

425. Tell me how he confounded the Jews who dwelt at Damascus, when he had not yet begun to work miracles.[107] How did he overcome the Greeks? Why was he sent to Tarsus?[108] Was it not because he mightily prevailed by his word, and pressed so hard upon them that not enduring their defeat, they were provoked even to kill him? For he had not yet begun to work miracles. Nor could any one say, that the multitude accounted him wonderful through the fame of his miracles, and that they who contended with him were daunted by the reputation of the man; for so far he conquered by his word alone.

426. How did he contend and dispute with those who endeavoured to Judaize in Antioch?[109] Did not the Areopagite who was of that most superstitious city, with his wife, follow him, because of his speech alone?[110] And how came Eutychus to fall from the window? Was it not because he protracted his discourse upon his doctrine to the dead of night?[111]

427. And what occurred at Thessalonica, and Corinth? What at Ephesus, and in Rome itself? Did he not consume whole days and nights in succession, upon expounding the Scriptures? Why should we mention his disputes with the Epicureans and Stoics?[112] for if I would reckon all, my speech would run to an excessive length.

428. Since then he appears to have made much use of his eloquence both before his miracles, and along with them, how will they yet venture to call unskilled him that was admired of all chiefly from his discourses and addresses?

429. Why did the Lycaonians suppose him to be Mercury? for that they were accounted gods, came of their miracles; but that he was Mercury was not owing to them, but to his discourse.

430. Wherein had this saint the prerogative over the other Apostles? And why throughout the world is he so much in the mouths of all? Why is he admired most of all, not among us alone, but among Jews and Greeks? Is it not because of the excellence of his epistles? by which he both profited, and will profit, not merely such as were believers then, but also those who have become such from that day to this, and those who are to be until the coming of Christ; nor will he ever cease to do this while the race of men endures.

---

107   Acts ix. 22.

108   Acts ix. 30.

109   Acts xv. 1-35; Gal. ii. 11.

110   Acts xvii. 34.

111   Acts xx. 9.

112   Acts xvii. 18.

431. For as a wall constructed of adamant, so his writings fortify the churches everywhere in the world. And like some noble chieftain, he stands even now among us, leading captive every thought unto the obedience of Christ, and casting down reasonings and every high thing which is exalted against the knowledge of God.[113] Now all this he does, by those admirable epistles which he has left us, full of divine wisdom.

432. Not for the overthrow of spurious doctrines alone, and the defence of the genuine, are his writings proper for us, but they contribute in the greatest degree, to our living aright. For our prelates, by using these even now, frame and fashion, and lead on to spiritual beauty, the chaste virgin which he betrothed to Christ.[114] By these they repel the diseases which threaten her, and preserve the health she gains. Such remedies has the unskilled one left us, and possessed of such virtue as they know well the proof of who employ them constantly!

433. That he himself gave great diligence in this matter, is from hence apparent.

VIII. S. Paul would have us excel in a similar manner.

434. Hear what he says in addressing his disciple: "Pay attention to reading, to exhortation, to doctrine;" and he mentions the fruit which proceeds from this: "For by doing this, thou wilt save both thyself and them that hear thee."[115] And again; "The servant of the Lord must not strive, but be gentle towards all men, apt to teach, forbearing."[116] And he proceeds to say, "But continue thou in what thou hast learned, and been assured of, knowing from whom thou hast learned them; and that from a child thou hast known the Holy Scriptures, which are able to make thee wise."[117] And again: "All Scripture is given by inspiration of God," he says, "and is profitable for doctrine, for reproof, for correction, for instruction in righteousness; that the man of God may be perfect."[118]

435. And hear also what he adds to Titus when discoursing upon the institution of bishops. "For," says he, "a bishop must hold fast the faithful word which is according to doctrine, that he may be able to convince gainsayers."[119]

436. How then will any one who is unskilful, as these say, be able to convince and silence gainsayers? What need is there to pay attention to reading and the Scriptures, if this unskilfulness is to be welcomed? Such things are an excuse and a subterfuge, and pretexts for idleness and sloth.

437. But he says these things are enjoined upon priests.

---

113 2 Cor. x. 5.

114 2 Cor. xi. 2.

115 1 Tim. iv. 13, 16.

116 2 Tim. ii. 24.

117 2 Tim. iii. 14, 15. The words 'unto salvation' are added in some editions.

118 2 Tim. iii. 16, 17.

119 Tit. i. 9.

438. And our discourse is now concerning priests. But it also applies to those who are subordinate; for hear again what he exhorts others to in another epistle: "Let the word of Christ dwell in you richly, in all wisdom."[120] And again: "Let your speech be always with grace, seasoned with salt, that ye may know how ye ought to answer every man;"[121] and "that they should be ready to give an answer" is spoken to all.[122] And writing to the Thessalonians he says: "Edify one another, as also ye do."[123]

439. And when he speaks of the priests: "Let the presbyters who rule well, be counted worthy of double honour, especially those who labour in word and doctrine."[124]

440. For this is the most perfect method of doctrine, when by what they do and what they say they conduct their disciples to the blessed life which Christ ordained. For doing is not sufficient for teaching.

441. And the saying is not mine, but that of the Saviour himself: for He says: "He that shall do and teach, the same shall be called great."[125] Now if doing were teaching, the second would be superfluous; and it would have sufficed merely to say, "He that shall do." But now by distinguishing both, he shows, that works are one thing, and words another, and each requires the other in order to perfect edification.

442. Do you not hear what the elect vessel of Christ says to the presbyters of the Ephesians? "Watch therefore; remembering that for three years night and day I ceased not with tears to admonish every one of you."[126] What need of tears or of admonition by words, with the Apostle's life so brilliant?

443. The one might contribute a great deal towards aiding us in performing the precepts; I would not affirm that the other by itself could accomplish everything.

IX. IF A PRIEST IS NOT ENDOWED WITH SUCH QUALIFICATIONS HE MUST NEEDS DO MUCH HARM TO HIS PEOPLE.

When contention arises about doctrines and all do battle out of the same Scriptures, what power will one's life exhibit in this case?

444. What will be the gain of his many struggles, if after all these toils one falls away through his great unskilfulness, and is severed from the body of the Church? This I know has been the fate of many. What will he profit by his endurance? Nothing; just as one will not (profit) by a sound faith, when his conduct is corrupt.

120   Col. iii. 16.

121   Col. iv. 6.

122   1 Thess. v. 11.

123   1 Pet. iii. 15.

124   1 Tim. v. 17.

125   Matt. v. 19.

126   Acts xx. 31.

445. For these reasons he ought to be pre-eminently experienced in those contests, who has been appointed to teach others.

446. For even if he himself remained in safety, and in nothing injured by gainsayers, still the multitude of more simple ones, ordered by him, when they saw their leader defeated, and having nothing to say to those who contradict, would lay the blame of his defeat, not upon his weakness, but on the unsoundness of his doctrine; and thus by the unskilfulness of one, much people is brought down to utter ruin. For even if they should not altogether be joined with the adversaries, they are nevertheless compelled to doubt of what they had to encourage them; and to that which they approached with an unfaltering faith, they are no longer able to adhere with the same stedfastness; but so much commotion occupies their souls through their teacher's defeat, that the evil ends in their shipwreck.

447. What ruin, and what fire he draws upon his unfortunate head, for each of those who perish, you have no need to learn from me; you well know it all.

448. Is it then from arrogance, is it through vainglory, that I would not be the cause of perdition to so many, and would not get to myself greater punishment, than what now awaits me yonder? Who would say so? No one, unless he would blame for nought, and philosophize over other's misfortunes.

Book V.

I. Public discourses require much labour and study.

449. I have sufficiently shown how much experience a teacher must have in contests for the truth. And I have besides something else to mention as the cause of ten thousand perils; or rather, I would not say *it* is the cause, but those who know not how to use it aright. Yet this very thing is the promoter of salvation and of many benefits, when it finds zealous and good men as its dispensers. What then is it? The great labour which should be expended upon public discourses to the people.

450. For, in the first place, the greater part of those who are placed under them, will not have regard to those who speak, as really teachers, but mistaking the position of disciples, they assume that of the lookers-on who are seated at worldly spectacles. And just as the multitude is there divided, and some attach themselves to this man and others to that; so also here, are they divided, and some follow one, and some another, hearing what is spoken in favour or in hate.

451. This is not the only annoyance; but there is another not inferior to it. For if it happens that any speaker should in his discourses interweave any thing which has been composed by others, he suffers more reproaches than those who plunder our possessions. And frequently when he has taken nothing from anybody, but is only suspected, he suffers the same as those who have been convicted. And why do I mention things composed by others? he cannot perpetually use his own productions.

452. The majority are wont to listen, not for profit, but for amusement, like those who sit in judgment on actors and musicians. Hence that ability to speak which we so lately repudiated, becomes more desirable here than to the very sophists when summoned to contend with one another.

II. He that is appointed to the Priesthood ought to despise applause, and to be a powerful speaker.

453. Here then is a demand for a noble soul, and one which far surpasses my mediocrity, in order to chastise this unruly and profitless pleasure of the multitude, and be able to divert their attention to something more beneficial: so that the people may follow and yield to him, and not he be led by their likings.

454. This however, can in no wise happen, except by these two means,—by despising applause, and by power in speaking.

455. If one of these should be wanting, that which remains becomes useless by being disjoined from the other. If he who despises applause, should not give out a

doctrine which is "with grace, and seasoned with salt,"[127] he is readily contemned by the many, and gains nothing by his nobleness of mind: but if he fairly succeeds in this respect, and yet happens to be overcome by the glory of plaudits, precisely the same mischief involves both him and the people; since he is more anxious to speak for the gratification of his hearers, than for their profit, owing to his love of praise.

456. And as he who is neither affected by commendation, nor skilled in speaking, does not yield to the pleasure of the crowd, nor can render them any benefit worth mentioning, through having nothing to say; so too, he who is carried away with desire for praise, and yet, while having ability to improve the multitude, instead of this, administers rather what shall please them—purchases therewith only the clamour of plaudits.

III. HE THAT HAS NOT BOTH THESE ENDOWMENTS WILL BE UNPROFITABLE TO THE PEOPLE.

457. The best kind of leader, then, must be strong in both respects; that the one may not be nullified by the other. When he stands up in public and would say what might disturb those who live at ease, and then stumbles and falters, and through lack of words is forced to blush, the benefit of what is spoken is utterly lost. For those who are rebuked, being vexed at what has been said, and having no other way to repel him, will visit him with mockery for his ignorance; supposing thereby to hide their own disgrace.

458. He, therefore, like some most skilful charioteer, must carefully proceed with both these virtues so that it may be possible for him to manage both aright. For when he is unrebukeable before all, he will then be able with what authority he will, both to chastise and to release all who are subject to his direction. But previously to this it will not be easy for him to do so.

459. But greatness of mind is not only to be displayed played in contempt for applause; it must reach further lest the benefit should be still incomplete.

IV. DETRACTION SHOULD ESPECIALLY BE TREATED WITH CONTEMPT.

What else then must he despise? Detraction and envy.

460. It is well neither immoderately to fear and dread, nor simply to overlook untimely accusations (and one in authority must needs endure unreasonable blame); but even if they are false, and are brought against us by common people, one must try to extinguish them at once.

461. For nothing will so increase a report, whether good or bad, as the unruly multitude: accustomed to hear and speak without examination, it will rashly utter all that reaches it, making no account of truth.

462. Therefore he must not disregard the multitude, but straightway put down base surmises when they originate, by persuading those who criminate others, though they should be the most unreasonable of men, and he must omit nothing which can remove an opinion that is not good. But if, when we have done every-

---

127 Col. iv. 6.

thing, those who find fault will not be persuaded, it will then be time to treat them with contempt. Therefore if one is immediately dejected by such accidents, he will never be able to effect anything noble and admirable; because sadness and constant cares are enough to prostrate the power of the soul, and to reduce it to extreme debility.

463. So that the priest ought to bear himself towards those that are subject to him, just as a father would towards very young children: as we take no notice when they complain, and strike, and lament; and even when they laugh and are pleased with us, we never think much about it; so is it with these, we are not to be lifted up by their praises, nor depressed by their scoldings, when they are uttered by them out of season.

464. This, my dear friend, is difficult, and, I fancy, even impossible.

465. For I know not whether it has been the character of any man not to rejoice when he is praised. And it is reasonable that he who rejoices should desire to enjoy the cause, and that he who desires to enjoy this, must in defect of it be absolutely distressed and troubled.[128]

466. For, as they who take pleasure in riches are sorrowful when they fall into poverty, and as they who have been accustomed to luxury cannot bear to live meanly, so also they who love applause are inwardly consumed as though by some famine, not only when they are censured without cause, but also while they are constantly lauded, and especially if they have been trained to this, or hear that others are commended.

V. THE LEARNED PRIEST REQUIRES MORE DILIGENCE THAN THE UNLEARNED.

467. What troubles and vexations, think you, will be his who enters upon the conflict of teaching with the desire of praise? It is not possible for the ocean ever to be free from waves, nor the soul of that man from cares and grief.

468. For even should one have great ability in speaking (and this is what we find in few), he is not on this account released from constant labour. For since speaking comes not by nature but by learning, although one may attain to perfection in it, he would certainly turn out destitute of it who did not cultivate the faculty with constant zeal and practice.

469. Therefore the greater labour falls to the more wise rather than to the more unlearned; for the evil is not the same to both if they are alike neglectful, but the difference is as great as the interval between their respective endowments.

470. Indeed, nobody would blame some men for producing nothing worthy of account; but there are others who are pursued by many accusations from everybody, unless they are continually producing what exceeds the estimation which all men have concerning them. Moreover, the former receive from everybody great praise for trifles; but what the latter do, unless it be amazing and astounding, is not only bereft of applause, but meets with many to blame it.

471. For listeners sit and judge, not by what is spoken, but by the reputation

---

128 According to another reading, the last clause may be rendered 'grieved and dejected, distressed and troubled.'

of speakers. So that when a man surpasses all in speaking, then most of all is indefatigable application required of him; for he is not allowed to have the common experience of human nature,—not to succeed in everything. And if what he says does not altogether accord with the great expectations of men, he goes away after receiving from many ten thousand scoffs and reproaches.

472. Nobody reasons with respect to him, that an attack of low spirits, pain, and care, and not seldom even anger, has obscured the brightness of intellect, and has not allowed its productions to come forth uneclipsed. Nobody considers at all, that as a man, it is not possible for him to be always the same, nor to succeed in everything; but that he will probably sometimes err, and appear inferior to his actual power. As I said, they will notice none of these things; but heap up accusations as if they sat in judgment upon an angel.

473. And, on the other hand, it is natural for a man to overlook the excellencies of his neighbour, even though they be many and great. But if a fault should happen to show itself, even though a common one, or occurring after a long time, it is quickly perceived, and forthwith laid hold of, and always remembered; and this trifling and insignificant thing has often injured the fame of many great men.

VI. THE JUDGMENT OF THE UNSKILFUL MULTITUDE IS NOT TO BE WHOLLY DESPISED, NOR ALTOGETHER REGARDED.

474. You see then, my excellent friend, that he especially who has ability to speak requires the greater care, and in addition to care, a measure of forbearance, which is not needed by all whom I have enumerated.

475. For many are perpetually rising up against him idly and without cause, and who have nothing to charge him with, except that they are annoyed that he is universally liked, and he is bound to bear their bitter calumny nobly.

476. For this accursed odium which they accumulate without cause, they cannot bear to conceal, and they reproach, and blame, and slander secretly, and are malicious openly: and the mind which began to be vexed and provoked by each of these, would not fail to be consumed by grief.

477. For they do not assail him themselves only, but they endeavour to do it by means of others; and oftentimes selecting some one of those who can say nothing, they exalt him with their praises, and admire him beyond his merit. Some do this through ignorance,[129] and others through both ignorance and envy, that they may take away the good name of the one, and not in order to exhibit as a wonderful person the other who is not such.

478. The noble-minded man will not have to contend with these alone, but oftentimes with the ignorance of an entire community. For it is impossible that a whole congregation should be made up of men of high attainments, but the larger portion of the Church usually consists of ordinary persons; the remainder are indeed wiser than these, but they have among them a far less proportion of such as can appreciate a discourse, than the general body have of wise men; and since there may exist but one or two who possess this ability, it necessarily comes to pass that he who speaks best carries away fewest acclamations; and there are times when he

---

129 For 'ignorance' some read 'madness.'

leaves with no applause whatever.

479. He must generously prepare himself for these inconsistencies, and forgive those who act thus from ignorance, and weep over those who permit this through envy, as wretched and pitiable; and not think that through either of them his ability has become smaller.

480. For if a most excellent painter, who surpassed all men in his art, should see a picture which had been painted with great accuracy laughed at by such as did not understand his art, he ought not to be dejected, and reckon his picture naught, through the judgment of those who did not appreciate it; just as he should not think a really worthless one to be something admirable and lovely because of the astonishment of the ignorant.

481. Let the best workman be himself the judge of his own works, and so reckon them good or bad as it may be; for the mind which contrived them pronounces the decision; and let him not suffer to enter his thoughts the opinion of strangers, when it is erroneous and unscientific.

VII. What is said should be prepared only with the view of pleasing God.

482. Let him therefore, who has undertaken the conflict of teaching, not give heed to the good reports of strangers, nor be cast down in spirit because of them; but composing his discourses so that he may please God; (and let this be his sole rule and plan for the best execution of them,—not plaudits, nor good reports;) if, indeed, he should also be praised by men, let him not repudiate their commendations; but if his hearers do not render them, let him neither seek for them, nor be vexed.

483. It will be to him a sufficient encouragement for his labours, and beyond them all, when he is conscious within himself, that he composes and arranges his doctrinal teaching with the view of pleasing God.

VIII. He who is not supremely indifferent to praise will be subject to many troubles.

484. If he should be overtaken with a desire for unreasonable praises, he will get no gain from his many labours, nor from his ability in speaking. For the soul which cannot endure the thoughtless accusations of the multitude is enervated, and abandons all diligence about speaking. Therefore we must be instructed chief of all to despise applause: for knowing how to speak is not sufficient for the preservation of the ability, unless the other (contempt of praise) be added.

485. But if any body would closely examine him that is not endowed with this faculty, he would discover him to lack contempt of praise no less than the other.

486. He will be impelled to many sins, who is overcome by popular opinion. For being incapable of equalling those of reputation in the art of speaking, he will not be loth to plot against them, to be jealous, to blame without cause, and to misbehave himself in many such ways; nay, he will venture everything, even though he must lose his own soul, to reduce their renown to the low level of his own insignificance.

487. And besides these things, he will stand aloof from the drudgery of labour, as though his soul were pervaded by torpidity. For that he should labour much

and receive small praise, is sufficient to cast and send into a deep sleep him that is unable to despise commendation. For the husbandman, when he tills a barren soil, and is forced to cultivate stony places, quickly desists from labouring, unless he has great earnestness in his work, or is pressed by fear of famine.

488. If they who are able to speak with much authority, require so much exertion to preserve their attainment, what difficulty, what trial, and what trouble will he be subject to, who has made no provision whatever, but is compelled to take anxious thought even in his exercises, that he may be able to bring together some little matter by great effort?

489. But if one of those who are associated with him, and occupy an inferior post, is able to make more display in this respect than he can; in such a case he has need of a soul in some sort divine, that he may not be led captive by envy, nor be subject to despondency. For that he who occupies a higher position should be surpassed by his inferiors, and yet bear it nobly, calls for no common and everyday soul, but one of adamant.

490. If he who gains the pre-eminence is gentle and moderate, the evil is in one way or another endurable; but if he is forward, ostentatious, and vain-glorious, the death of the one will be daily desirable, so bitter will the other render his life, by openly spurning him, secretly ridiculing him, derogating much from his authority, and wishing himself to be everybody; and his greatest security in all this will be the freedom he has acquired in speaking, the zeal of the multitude respecting him, and the affection of all his subordinates.

491. Know you not how great a love of preaching at present possesses the souls of Christians; and that they who exercise themselves herein are chiefly held in honour, not only by those who are without, but by the household of faith?

492. How then can any one endure such a disgrace as that all should be blank silence when he speaks, and think it an annoyance, and expect the end of the discourse like a rest from their labours, and yet, that when another speaks at any length, they should hear him cheerfully, and be sorry when he is about to conclude, and be vexed when he wishes to be silent?

493. Although these things may appear to you trifling and despicable, because you are inexperienced, still they are enough to extinguish the promptitude, and relax the energy of the soul, unless one should dispossess himself of all human affections, and study to become like those incorporeal powers, which are haunted neither by envy nor love of glory, nor any similar disorder.

494. If, therefore, any man is such as to be able to subjugate popular applause, that wild beast so difficult to overtake, so hard to defeat, and so untameable, and to cut off its many heads, or rather not to allow them even to grow, he will be able easily to repel many other assaults, and to enjoy a peaceful haven. But while he is not delivered from this, he will sow broadcast in his soul, a multifarious war, constant trouble, dejection, and a host of other emotions.

495. What need have I to enumerate remaining difficulties, which nobody will be able to name or to understand, save he who is engaged in these affairs?

Book VI.

I. Priests are liable to correction for the sins of other men.

496. The things which pertain to the present are such as you have heard; but how shall we endure those of the future, when we are compelled to render an account for every one of those who have been committed to us? for the loss consists not in shame alone, but eternal punishment ensues.

497. For although I have mentioned it before, I will not even now be silent respecting this:—"Obey them that have the rule over you, and submit yourselves; for they watch for your souls as they that must give an account;"[130] because the fear of this warning would continually agitate my soul.

498. For if it were better that a millstone were hanged about his neck, and that he were drowned in the sea, who offends one alone, even the least;[131] and all who wound the conscience of their brethren sin against Christ himself,—what shall they suffer, and what punishment will befall them, who destroy not only one, or two, or three, but so many multitudes?[132]

499. For they cannot ascribe it to inexperience, nor take refuge in ignorance, nor pretend necessity and compulsion. It would rather be possible for one of their subordinates, if any, to avail himself of this refuge for his personal sins, than for those who bear rule to do so for the sins of others.

500. Why so? Because he who has been appointed to correct the follies of others, and to forewarn them of their coming war with the devil, cannot pretend ignorance, nor say, "I heard not the trumpet; I foresaw not the war."

501. For this has he been stationed, as Ezekiel says, that he may sound an alarm to others, and forewarn them of coming troubles; and therefore, punishment is unavoidable if so much as one should perish. For he says, "If when the sword comes, the watchman blow not the trumpet for the people, nor give them notice, and the sword come and take any soul, it is taken because of its iniquity, it is true, but its blood will I require of the watchman."[133]

502. Cease then to thrust me on to so inevitable a judgment.

503. For our concern is not about a generalship, nor a kingdom, but about a matter which demands angelic virtue.

---

130 Heb. xiii. 17.

131 Matt. xviii. 6.

132 1 Cor. viii. 11, 12.

133 Ezek. xxxiii. 6.

II. Priests require to be more circumspect than monks.

504. The soul of the priest should be purer than the very solar rays, that the Holy Spirit may never leave him desolate, and that he may be able to say "I live; yet not I, but Christ liveth in me."[134]

505. For if they who dwell in solitude, and are not engaged in the city and the forum and their troubles, and enjoy continually the haven and a calm, will not put confidence in the security of such a mode of life, but provide a multitude of other protections, defending themselves all around; and are anxious to say and do all things very correctly, that they may draw nigh to God with assurance and unsullied purity, as far as man can do; what power and strength, think you, does the priest require, that he may keep his soul free from all defilement, and preserve its spiritual beauty unmarred?

506. Much greater purity is demanded of him than of them; and as more is demanded of him, he is more exposed than they are to necessary influences which must contaminate him, if he did not render his soul inaccessible to them by exercising constant denial and great firmness.

507. Handsome faces and delicate motions, an affected gait and a mincing voice, painted eyes and tinted cheeks, an array of tresses and dyed locks, sumptuous garments and variety of golden ornaments, beautiful jewels, sweetness of perfumes, and all that the female sex affects, are enough to agitate the mind when it is not mortified by great and wise austerity.

508. That a man should be disturbed by these things is nothing wonderful; but that the devil should be able to smite and shoot down the souls of men by what is quite the reverse of them, is a circumstance fraught with wonder and difficulty. For some who have avoided these snares have actually been caught in those which are very different from them. Even a neglected face and untended hair, sordid apparel and a slovenly appearance, homely manners and simple utterance, unstudied gait and unaffected voice, living in penury, and being despised, unpatronised, and in solitude, have first led the beholder to pity, and then to utter ruin.

III. The monk is less embarrassed than the man who rules in the church.

Many who escaped the former nets, which are woven of gold and perfumes and garments, and the other things I mentioned, have easily stumbled into those which are so different from them, and have perished.

509. Since then, both by penury and wealth, by adorning and a neglected appearance, by manners studied and unstudied, and, in a word, by all that I have enumerated, war is enkindled in the soul of a beholder, and its machinations encompass him on every side, where can he find breathing room, while so many snares surround him? What retreat can he discover, I say not to avoid being taken by force, for this is not so difficult, but that he may preserve his soul untroubled by defiling thoughts?

510. Honours which are the causes of ten thousand mischiefs, I pass over.

---

134 Gal. ii. 20.

511. For those which come from women are ruinous to the maintenance of sobriety, and often cast down him who does not know how to watch continually against such temptations.

512. As for the honours which come from men, unless one receives them with much dignity he is ensnared by two contrary affections, by the servility of flattery, and the folly of conceit. He is forced to stoop to those who favour him, and is inflated against the lesser brethren because of the honours which others have given him, and is hurried into the whirlpool of arrogance.

513. These things I say indeed, but what injury they cause, nobody can thoroughly learn without experience; for not these things alone, but more and worse than these must needs befall men who are engaged in public life.

514. But he who courts a solitude enjoys immunity from them all; and if some absurd imagining should ever represent any such thing to him, still it is a feeble fancy and can soon be extinguished, because his eyes find no fuel outside to feed the flame.

515. The monk, too, fears for himself alone; and even when he is compelled to care for others also, they are very few; and if they were more, they are fewer than those who attend the churches, and bring lighter cares by far to him that is set over them, not simply because of their fewness, but because they are all exempt from worldly affairs, and have neither children, nor wife, nor anything of that sort to be anxious for; and this makes them very obedient to their directors, and to have a common residence; so that their faults can be carefully watched and corrected, by the constant oversight of the teacher, which tends no little to progress in virtue.

IV. THE PRIEST IS ENTRUSTED WITH AUTHORITY OVER THE WORLD, AND WITH OTHER SOLEMN DUTIES.

516. Most of those who are placed under the priest, are fettered by worldly cares, and this makes them more sluggish in the performance of spiritual duties. It is therefore necessary for the teacher to sow every day, if I may thus speak, in order that by his perseverance the word of doctrine may be retained by those who hear it. For a load of wealth, greatness of influence, the indifference which springs from luxury, and many other things besides, choke the seed scattered, aud oftentimes the abundance of thorns does not allow what is sown to fall even to the surface of the earth.[135] And then, excess of trouble, pressure from poverty, constant afflictions, and other such things contrary to the foregoing, divert men from anxiety after divine affairs; and not even the smallest fraction of their people's sins can become visible to them. And how should they, when they do not know most of them even by sight?

517. Such is the difficulty which the concerns of the people cause him; and if any one were to search into things which pertain to God, he would discover the others to be as nothing, so much more great and diligent is the care which these demand.

518. What a man ought he to be who is ambassador for a whole city! and why do I say, for a city?—for ail the world! and who prays that God will be propitious

---

135 Matt. xiii. 1-23; 1 Cor. iii. 5-9.

to the sins of all men, not of the living only, but of the departed? I do not think the boldness of speech of Moses and of Elijah, by any means adequate to such supplication. For he draws nigh to God, as though the whole world were committed to his care, and he himself the father of all men, praying that wars may be extinguished everywhere, and that troubles may be brought to an end, and entreating for every man peace and prosperity, and speedy deliverance from impending evils, both privately and publicly. And he must in all things excel all for whom he prays, as much as the ruler must excel the ruled.

519. If he has invoked the Holy Ghost, and performed that most awful sacrifice, and constantly touched with his hands the common Lord of all, tell me, where we shall rank him? What purity and what piety shall we demand of him? for consider what his hands ought to be which minister these things! What his tongue, which utters such words! and what should be so pure and holy as his soul which receives so great a Spirit!

520. Angels are then present with the priest, and the whole tribune and space around the altar is filled with heavenly powers in honour of Him that is there.[136]

521. And this may be believed in consequence of what is then celebrated. I once heard somebody relate, that an aged and excellent man who was accustomed to witness revelations, told him he had been counted worthy of such a vision, and on that occasion had suddenly seen a multitude of angels, (as far as it was possible for him to do so) clothed in glittering robes, surrounding the altar, and bowing down, as one might see soldiers who stand where the king is present; and I believe it.

522. Another told me, not what he learned from somebody else, but was himself privileged both to see and hear of those who are about to depart hence that,—if they partake of the sacraments with a pure conscience,—when they are going to expire, angels keep guard over them because of that which they have received, and take them away.

523. Do you never shudder when you admit a soul to so sacred a function, and raise to the dignity of priests him that was clothed in defiled raiment, and was excluded by Christ from the remainder of the guests?[137]

524. As a light which lightens all the world, ought the soul of a priest to shine. But mine, has so much darkness surrounding it, through an evil conscience, that it is always depressed, and never able to look at its Master with boldness.

525. Priests are the salt of the earth; but who would easily bear with my folly and inexperience in all things, except you who have been wont to love me to excess?

526. For (a priest) ought not only to be thus pure, seeing he is counted worthy of such a ministry, but also very wise, and experienced in many things; and he ought to understand all worldly matters no less than those who are engaged in them, and to be separated from them all more than the monks who occupy the

---

136 There are other readings and renderings of the latter half of this sentence, but that which is given above appears to be the true one. The 'tribune' or # Greek"# βῆμα# /Greek# , otherwise called the 'choir' and 'sanctuary,' is the space right and left of the altar, reserved for the ministrants and clergy. It differs from the reader's # i# ambo, bema# /i# , or # i# desk# /i# , which was in the nave of the church and not in the chancel.

137 Matt. xxii. 13.

mountains.

527. For since he must converse with men who have wives, bring up children, possess servants, are surrounded with great wealth, discharge public functions, and are in power, he ought to be accommodating.[138]

528. Accommodating, I say, not disingenuous, not a flatterer and a hypocrite, but endued with much freedom and boldness, and understanding how to adapt himself with advantage, when the state of affairs requires it, and to be at the same time kind and severe.

529. For one method is not to be followed with all who are under authority; because it would not do for physicians to prescribe to all their patients according to one rule, or for a pilot to know but one way of contending with the winds;—and constant storms beset this ship as well. But these storms assail not only from without, but spring up even within; and there is need both of much condescension and strictness.

V. THE PRIEST MUST BE QUALIFIED FOR EVERYTHING.

530. All these different things look to one end,—the glory of God, and the edification of the Church.

531. Great is the struggle of the monks, and much their labour; but if one should compare their toils with the priestly office when well administered, he would find the difference as great as the distance between a private person and a king.

532. For although in the former case, there is much fatigue, the contest is common to body and soul alike, or rather is mostly accomplished in the discipline of the body; and if it should not be strong, the willing mind remains, though it is unable to proceed to action. Continual fasting, sleeping on the ground, vigils, neglect of ablution, much toil, and other things which tend to the affliction of the body, all cease when the body which is to be chastised is not strong enough.

533. But in this case the discipline is purely that of the soul, and no vigour of body is required in order to display its virtue. For how does strength of body help us to be neither self-sufficient, irascible, nor headstrong, but sober and prudent, decorous, and everything else wherewith S. Paul rendered perfect his image of the best of priests?[139]

534. But nobody could have this to say of the virtue of a monk. Wonder-workers have need of many instruments, such as wheels, ropes, and swords; but a philosopher has all his skill in his mind, requiring nothing external.

535. So here, the monk requires a good bodily constitution, and places adapted for his mode of life,—that they be not too far removed from converse with men, and may yet possess the retirement of solitude, and moreover, may not lack the best temperature of the seasons, because nothing is so insupportable to one who macerates himself with fastings, as a variable climate. I need say nothing here about the supply of clothing and diet, which are matters they must attend to, endeavouring

---

138 The quality denoted is that versatility to which S. Paul refers in 1 Cor. ix. 22, 'I am made all things to all men.'

139 1 Tim. iii. 2-7.

to do everything for themselves.

VI. TO RULE WELL IN THE CHURCH IS A GREATER PROOF OF ENDURANCE THAN TO BE A MONK.

536. Now the priest will require to attend to none of these things on his own account; but is unoccupied by trifles, and takes his part in everything which is not injurious, having all his wisdom stored in the treasuries of his soul.

537. If any one should admire those who live alone and avoid converse with the many, I should say myself, it was a token of self-endurance, but not a sufficient evidence of all virtue in the soul. For he who sits at the helm in port, gives no strict proof of his capability; but nobody would deny him to be an excellent steersman who could save the vessel in the ocean and in the midst of a storm.

538. Therefore I should not say that a monk is to be excessively and inordinately admired, because he has nothing to disturb him, while he remains in solitude, and the sins he commits are neither many nor great; for he has nothing to incite and stir up his soul.

VII. HE WHO LIVES APART, AND HE WHO LEADS A PUBLIC LIFE HAVE DIFFERENT CARES.

But if a man has committed himself to whole multitudes, and is compelled to bear the sins of many, and yet remains unwavering and firm, guiding his soul in the storm as in the calm, he is the man to be justly applauded and admired of all; for he has displayed sufficient proof of personal excellence.

539. Wonder not then, if I, who abandon the forum, and popular assemblies, have not many accusers.

540. For nobody ought to wonder, if I sinned not while asleep, if I fell not when I did not wrestle, and if I received no wound when I did not fight.

541. Who, tell me, who will be able to speak against me, and to reveal any depravity? Will this roof or this room? Nay; they cannot utter a sound.

542. Will my mother, who knows me better than all? With her especially I am not in league, neither have we ever come to a quarrel. But even if this had happened, no mother is so callous and without love to her children, as to calumniate and slander before all men, him she travailed with, and bore, and reared, if no occasion compelled her, or nothing forced her.

543. Nevertheless, if any one should subject my soul to a careful test, he would find many things corrupt in it; and you who most of all are accustomed to extol me with your encomiums are aware of this.

544. I do not say these things now to depreciate myself; for recollect how often I have said to you, when similar conversation has frequently arisen: "If any one gave me the option to choose, where I would rather be distinguished, in the government of the Church or in the monastic life, I should prefer the former ten thousand times over;" and I have never ceased to eulogize to you those who were able to fill the ministerial office well. And everybody will admit that I should not have avoided what I eulogized if I had felt equal to its duties.

545. But what was I to do? Nothing is so profitless for the governance of the

Church, as this sloth and lukewarmness, which others consider to be a sort of discipline, but which I regard as a veil for my own worthlessness, enveloping in it most of my shortcomings, and not letting them appear.

546. He that has been accustomed to enjoy so much freedom from occupation, and to live in great quiet, even though he be of a noble nature, is disturbed and troubled by his inexperience, and his want of practice removes no small portion of his personal ability; and if he is at one and the same time of slow understanding, and inexpert in such contests (which is just my position), he would be in no wise better than men of stone, if he accepted this stewardship.

547. For this cause few of those who come into these contests out of the monastic arena become conspicuous; but most of them betray themselves, and stumble, and their experience is unpleasant and painful. This is to be looked for; for if one's contests and exercises are not of the same description (as he has been used to), he that contends is no better off than those who are undisciplined.

548. He who comes into this arena ought especially to despise glory, to be superior to anger, and to be filled with much wisdom; but no opportunity for training is supplied to him who affects the monastic life; for he neither has many to stimulate him to be careful to chasten the power of wrath; nor those who admire and applaud him, that he may learn to despise the praise of the multitude; while the wisdom which is required in the churches is of no great account with monks. When, therefore, they come into contests, of which they have not been careful to get experience, they are at a loss, they are in a maze, they fall into embarrassment, and, besides making no progress towards success, many oftentimes lose what they possessed when they came forward.

VIII. IT IS MORE EASY FOR SUCH AS DWELL APART TO PRACTISE VIRTUE, THAN FOR SUCH AS HAVE THE CARE OF MANY.

[BASIL.] 549. What then? Shall we appoint to the stewardship of the Church, those who are engaged in public, who are anxious about worldly things, who are veterans in contention and railing, who are endued with boundless craft, and are accustomed to luxury?

[CHRYSOSTOM.] 550. Far from it, my excellent friend, said I, such men should never enter our thoughts when the question of priests arises, but only he who, while conversing and occupied with all men, is able to preserve more simple and unshaken than monks themselves, purity and serenity, sanctity, patience, and sobriety, and all other good qualities which monks possess.

551. Thus he who has many defects is able to conceal them by solitude, and to render them inert by associating himself with nobody; but when he comes into public, all he obtains is to become ridiculous, and he runs into greater danger.

552. The same almost would have befallen me, if the providence of God had not quickly restrained the fire from my head.

553. It is not possible that one in this condition should be concealed when he is placed in public, but all is then detected; and as the fire tries metallic substances, so the test to which the clergy are put indicates what the souls of the men are; so that if a man is irascible, or pusillanimous, or arrogant, or boastful, or anything else, this

reveals it all, and speedily exposes his vices.

554. Not only does it expose his vices, it renders them worse and more powerful. Even the wounds of the body when chafed become more difficult to heal; and the passions of the soul when stimulated and excited commonly become more violent, and urge their possessors to transgress the more.

555. They carry away him that is heedless, to love of praise, haughtiness, and the desire of wealth; and they drag him into luxury, licence, indifference, and gradually into evils worse than these, and which are produced by them.

556. There are many things in the way which can paralyze the soul's activity, and hinder its straightforward career.[140]

557. First of all there is conversation with women. For he who is in authority, and cares for all his flock, must not be concerned for the division containing the men, and overlook that of the women, which urgently requires more forethought, because it easily lapses into sin; wherefore he that has been appointed to administer the office of a bishop is required to be, if not more so, at least in an equal measure solicitous for their health. For he must visit the sick, comfort the sorrowful, chide the negligent, and help the afflicted.

558. Upon such occasions the evil one would discover many avenues of approach, if a man did not fortify himself by very careful custody. For the eye wounds and troubles the soul; not merely the eye of a wanton woman, but even that of a prudent one; flatteries also render men susceptible, and esteem enslaves them, while fervent love—the cause of all good things—becomes the cause of countless evils to those who use it not aright.

559. And it has occurred that constant solicitude has blunted acuteness of perception, and rendered the bird[141] more heavy than lead; while anger, coming down like smoke, has occupied the whole inner man.

560. Why should I mention the mischiefs which result from grief,[142] reproaches, insults, and rebukes, from superiors and from inferiors, from wise and from unwise?

IX. POPULAR SUSPICION IS NOT TO BE TREATED WITH CONTEMPT EVEN WHEN UNFOUNDED.

561. That class which is destitute of right judgment is especially querulous, and would never readily allow a vindication.

562. But "he that rules well"[143] is obliged not to despise even these, but to explain to all the things whereof they accuse him, with much gentleness and meekness, rather forgiving their unreasonable blame than becoming indignant and angry.

563. For if the blessed Paul feared lest he should incur the suspicion of theft

---

140 Instead of "straightforward career," another reading gives "career towards God."

141 "The bird," that is, the soul. Compare Ps. lv. 6.

142 According to a different reading "the mischiefs which remain."

143 1 Tim. v. 17.

among the disciples, and therefore admitted others to the ministration of the funds, saying, "That no man may blame us in this abundance which is administered by us,"[144] ought not we to make every effort to remove evil suspicions, even when they are really *false* and unreasonable, and at the farthest distance from our thought?

564. We are not so far removed from any sin as Paul was from theft, and yet, notwithstanding he was so remote from this evil deed, he was not therefore indifferent to the suspicion of the multitude, although it was exceedingly unreasonable and insane. For it was madness to cherish any such suspicion of that blessed and admirable person. But he nevertheless puts far away even the occasions of this so irrational suspicion, and which no one would have entertained who was not stark mad. He did not treat with disdain the folly of the multitude, neither did he say, "Whoever could have cherished such surmises about me, when all men honour and admire me on account of my miracles, and my integrity of life?" Quite the contrary; he both foresaw and anticipated this base suspicion, and plucked it up by the roots, or rather did not let it begin to grow. Why so? "Because," said he, "we provide things honest," not only before the Lord, but also "before men."[145]

565. So much diligence must be used, or rather, even more, not only to put down and restrain floating rumours which are not good, but to look forward from afar to where they may originate, and to remove beforehand the pretexts from which they spring; not to wait till they assume consistency, and are put into circulation by the mouths of the multitude, for then it will not be easy to extinguish them finally, but very difficult and perhaps even impossible, and in no case without mischief, because the attempt is made after many have been injured.

566. But how long shall I continue in pursuit of what is unattainable? For to enumerate all the difficulties here, is nothing else than measuring an ocean.

567. Even if one should become free from every passion (which is an impossibility), that he might rectify the failings of others, he would be compelled to endure innumerable ills. When you have added his personal infirmities, behold an abyss of toils and cares, and what he must suffer who is anxious to overcome his own and others' faults!

X. It is no great matter to save one oneself.

[Basil.] 568. And now, said he, have you no need of toils, and have you no cares, while you keep to yourself?

[Chrysostom.] I have indeed, said I, even now.

569. For how can it be, that one who is a man and lives this much-vexed life should be released from cares and conflict? But it is not the same thing to enter upon a vast ocean and to row across a river; and such is the distance between these cares and the others.

570. Now, indeed, I should wish to be useful to others, if I could, and this to me is a matter of much prayer. But if I cannot profit another, provided it happen that I should save myself and escape from the tempest, I shall be satisfied with this.

---

144 2 Cor. viii. 20.

145 Rom. xii. 17.

[BASIL.] 571. Then you think this to be a great matter, said he; but do you think you can be saved at all, if you are useful to nobody else?

[CHRYSOSTOM.] 572. You have spoken well and right, said I, for I do not believe that he can be saved who does not labour for the salvation of his neighbour. It profited that wretched servant nothing that he had not diminished his talent, but he perished through not increasing it and returning twofold.[146]

573. But still, I think a lighter punishment will descend on me when I am called to account for not saving others too, than if it were for destroying others as well as myself by turning out much worse after so great an honour. I believe I shall now suffer as much punishment as the magnitude of my sins demands; whereas, after accepting this office, it would not be double merely, or threefold, but manifold, through causing a greater number to stumble, and, after receiving greater honours, offending the God that honoured me.

XI. A FAR SEVERER PUNISHMENT AWAITS THE SINS OF PRIESTS THAN THOSE OF COMMON MEN.

574. Therefore by accusing the Israelites more vehemently, He shows that they were deserving of greater chastisement through sinning after so many honours had come to them from Him; at one time saying, "I have known of all the tribes of the earth only you; therefore will I be avenged upon you for your iniquities:"[147] And at another time, "I took of your sons for prophets, and of your young men for sanctification."[148]

575. And earlier than the prophets, willing to show that sins receive a far greater punishment when committed by priests than when by private persons, He ordains as great a sacrifice to be offered for the priests as for all the people.[149] Now this signifies nothing else than that the wounds of a priest require greater assistance, as much indeed as those of all the people: but they would not require more if they were not worse. And they are worse, not of their own nature, but through the dignity of the priest who presumes to do that which lies heavy upon him.

576. And why do I speak of the men who follow this ministration? For the daughters of the priests, who have no part in the priestly office, yet on account of their father's dignity suffer a much severer punishment for their sins.[150] Their transgression and that of the daughters of private persons is equal indeed, for both are fornication, but the punishment of the one is far more severe than that of the others.[151]

146 Matt. xxv. 24.

147 Amos iii. 2.

148 Amos ii. 11.

149 Lev. iv. 3-21.

150 Lev. xxi. 9.

151 Deut. xxii. 13–24.

XII. Examples to show that sorrow and fear are caused by the anticipation of the priestly office.

You see then how abundantly God declares that he exacts a far greater penalty from the ruler than from the ruled. For He who punishes more than others the daughter of a priest on his account, will by no means inflict upon him who is the cause of additional torments to her, the same punishment as upon others, but one far greater.

577. And assuredly this is right. For the mischief does not involve merely himself, but casts down the souls of the more feeble and of such as look up to him.

578. Ezekiel also, wishing to show this, distinguishes between the judgment of the rams and that of the sheep.

579. Do you not think I had reason to cherish fear? For in addition to what has been mentioned, although much effort is required of me even now that I be not altogether mastered by the passions of my soul, nevertheless I endure the toils, and fly not from the contest.

580. Even now indeed, I am liable to be caught by vain-glory, but I often recover myself, and I understand that I am caught, and sometimes also I rebuke my soul which has been enslaved.

581. Even now unreasonable desires assail me, but they kindle a feebler flame, for my outward eyes cannot obtain fuel for the fire.

582. I am altogether exempt from speaking ill of any one, and of hearing him spoken ill of when none are present to converse with me, for these walls cannot utter a word.

583. But I cannot similarly avoid anger, even when there are none to provoke me; for oftentimes the recollection of unreasonable men, and of what is done by them comes over me, and causes my heart to swell, but not in an extreme degree, for I at once subdue its commotion, and persuade it to be quiet, by saying, it is a great calamity and extremely wretched to neglect one's own faults, and to be busied about those of my neighbours. But if I came among the multitude, and were involved in countless excitements, I should not be able to profit by this admonition, nor to find considerations for my instruction.

584. But as they who are thrust down precipices by some torrent or otherwise, can foresee the destruction in which they will come to an end, but can discover no assistance, so if I should fall into a great tumult of passions, I could see my punishment increasing every day, but I could not as now control myself, and it would no longer be easy for me as before to rebuke those afflictions which would rage on every side.

585. For my mind is weak and small, and easily conquered, not only by these affections, but by envy the most bitter of all, and it knows not how to bear with moderation either rebuffs or honours, but it is excessively lifted up by the latter, and cast down by the former.

586. Therefore, as wild beasts while in health and vigour, prevail over those who attack them, especially if they are weak and unskilful, but if any one should macerate them by hunger, he would appease their fury, and extinguish most of their strength, so that even he who is not very courageous might undertake a contest and war against them; so is it with the affections of the soul,—he who renders

them feeble subjects them to right reason, but he who carefully cherishes them, ordains for himself a fiercer battle with them, and renders them so terrible that he lives all his time in bondage and in fear.

587. What then is the food of these wild beasts? — of vain-glory, honours and praises; of pride, greatness of power and authority; of envy, the good fame of neighbours; of avarice, the liberality of the benevolent; of intemperance, luxury and constant interviews with women; and so of the rest.

588. Now if I come into public life all these will assail me, rend my soul, be a terror to me, and cause my war with them to be more difficult. And even while I remain in private they will be subdued only with great violence; but still, by the grace of God they will be subdued, and nothing will be left to them but their howling.

589. For these reasons I keep to this domicile, I do not go out, I keep no company, I have no associates, and I bear to hear a thousand rebukes which I would gladly clear away, and am pained and grieved because I cannot. For it would not be easy for me to be conversant with men, and at the same time to abide in my present security. Wherefore I beseech you to pity rather than scold one who is involved in so great a difficulty.

590. But I have not persuaded you yet. It remains therefore that I should make known to you that which alone I have left unspoken. Perhaps indeed, it will seem incredible to many, but I shall not on this account feel ashamed to bring it forward. If what I say is proof of an evil conscience, and of innumerable sins, yet since God, who is to judge me, knows all things perfectly, what more can befall me through the ignorance of men?

591. What then is it which I have left unspoken? From the very day on which you aroused in me this apprehension,[152] my body has often been in peril of complete dissolution, so great the fear, and so great the sorrow which possessed my soul.

592. For considering the glory of the Spouse of Christ, her holiness, her spiritual beauty, her wisdom, and her comeliness, and meditating upon my own failings, I have never ceased to lament over both her and myself; and constantly groaning and perplexed I have said to myself:

593. Who then has counselled this? Wherein has the Church of God sinned so much? What has so provoked her Lord that she should be committed to me the most unworthy of all, and should sustain so much disgrace?

594. Often reasoning thus with myself, and unable to bear even the idea of anything so wrong, I have lain speechless like men paralyzed, and able neither to hear nor see. When this great prostration has left me, for it has sometimes been intermitted, tears and sorrow have succeeded, and after an abundance of tears, fear has again occupied me, troubling, disturbing, and agitating my mind.

595. In such tumult have I spent the time which has elapsed. But you knew it not, and thought I lived in peace. Well, I will now try to reveal to you the tempest of my soul; for you will perhaps dismiss your accusations, and at length forgive me. How then pray, how shall I discover it to you? If you would see it clearly, there is no other course than that I should lay my very heart bare. But because this cannot be, I will endeavour as well as I can to describe to you by some faint image the shadow

---

152 Namely, that I was to be made a priest.

of my grief; but from that image infer my grief alone.

596. Let us suppose that the betrothed of any one is the daughter of the king of all that lies beneath the sun; that this damsel has indescribable beauty, transcending that of human nature, and herein surpassing by a long interval the whole race of women; that she has such virtue of soul as to leave very far behind the entire race of men, both those who are and those who ever shall be; that she excels all the rules of philosophy in the comeliness of her manners, and that she eclipses all the grace of her person by the loveliness of her countenance.

597. (Let us suppose) her suitor not to be enamoured of the virgin on these accounts alone, but to have affection for her irrespectively of them, and that in his passion he outvies the most infatuated lovers that ever were.

598. Then (let us suppose) that while he is inflamed by this charm, he hears somehow that the admired and loved one is about to be taken in marriage by some mean reprobate of low condition, deformed in person, and the most wretched of all who live.

599. Have I suggested to you some small portion of my sorrow? Is it enough to conclude my comparison here? With respect to my *grief* I think it is enough; and for this cause only have I introduced it. But that I may show you the measure of my *fear* and *astonishment*, let me again proceed to another picture.

600. Let there be an armament consisting of infantry, and cavalry, and marines: let a multitude of ships cover the sea; and let the phalanxes of infantry and cavalry cover many plains and the tops of the mountains:

601. Let their brazen weapons flash in the sun, and let the glittering of their helmets and spears be reflected by the beams which they emit: let the clashing of the spears, and the neighing of the horses be borne to heaven itself: let neither land nor sea be visible, but brass and steel everywhere.

602. Let enemies be arrayed against them,—men wild and fierce; and let the hour of conflict be imminent.

603. Then let some one seize at once a stripling from among those brought up in the country, and understanding nothing but a shepherd's pipe and crook; and let him be armed with brazen armour.

604. Let him be led round all the host, and shown the battalions and their officers, the archers, the slingers, the captains, the generals, the infantry, the cavalry, the spearmen, the ships and their commanders, the marines thronging on board; and the multitude of warlike engines stored in the vessels.

605. Let him see the whole battle array of the enemy, and their dreadful aspect, the extraordinary supply and countless number of their weapons, the ravines, and steep precipices, and the ruggedness of the mountains.

606. Let him see among the enemies horses flying by some enchantment, and infantry carried through the air, and the power and form of every kind of sorcery.

607. Let him reckon up the accidents of war, the cloud of arrows, the shower of darts, the great mist and obscurity, the darkest night—which the multitude of missiles causes, hiding by their numbers the solar rays,—the dust which blinds men's eyes not less than darkness itself, the torrents of blood, the groans of the fallen, the shouts of the surviving, the heaps of the prostrate, wheels baptized with blood, horses with their riders thrown headlong down by the multitude of those who lie

dead, the ground with everything in confusion,—blood, bows, and darts, horses' hoofs and men's heads lying together, an arm and a wheel, a greave and a cloven breast, brains besmeared on swords, the point of a spear broken off, and with an eye transfixed upon it!

608. Let him then enumerate the sufferings of the fleet,—ships burning in the midst of the waters, and sinking with their soldiery, the roar of the waters, the clamour of the sailors, the shouting of the soldiers, the foam mixed up of waves and blood, and at the same time dashing into all the ships,—the dead upon the decks, the drowning, the swimming, dashed upon the rocks, swallowed up by the waves, and obstructing the courses of the vessels.

609. And when such a one has carefully learned all the horrors of war, let him add thereto the terrors of bondage, and slavery worse than any death.

610. When he has been told all this, let him be bidden forthwith to mount his horse, and command all that armament.

611. Think you the stripling could bear the lesson merely, and would not lose heart at once and at the first glance?

XIII. OUR CONFLICT WITH THE DEVIL IS MORE GRIEVOUS THAN ANY OTHER.

612. Do not think I overstrain the matter by what I say, nor suppose that my words are exaggerated; because we can see none of the things which are invisible, while we are enclosed in this body as in some prison. For you would witness a conflict far greater and more dreadful than this, if with these eyes of yours, you could ever see the devil's most dark array and mad attack.

613. For neither brass nor steel are there, nor horses and chariots and wheels, nor fire and arrows, which are visible; but other engines far more dire than they. These are enemies who need not breastplate and shield, nor swords and spears; but the sight alone of the accursed host suffices to paralyze the soul, unless it is most nobly constituted, and enjoys much foresight from God, before it is called personal labour.

614. And if it were possible, that having put off this body, or while being in the body, you could clearly and fearlessly witness all his array and war against us, you would see, not torrents of blood, nor dead bodies, but so many corpses of souls, and wounds so dreadful, that you would think to be mere child's play and sport rather than war, the whole picture of war which I have just gone over with you, so many are there smitten every day.

615. But the wounds are not fatal in the same sense in the two cases, but as far as the soul is above the body, so wide is the difference of the one death from the other. For when the soul receives a wound and falls, it does not lie insensible, as the body does, but being gnawed by an evil conscience is now henceforward tormented, and after its removal hence, at the time of judgment, it is delivered to undying vengeance. Now if any one should be without sorrow for the wounds inflicted by the devil, his misery becomes the greater for his insensibility. For he who is not pained by a first wound will readily receive a second, and after that another; because the wicked one will not cease smiting until the last breath, when he finds a

soul supine and disregarding previous strokes.

616. If you would inquire into the manner of attacking, you would find it more violent and varied here; for no one knows so many forms of fraud and guile as that wicked one, (whereby he acquires the greater influence), nor can any person have such implacable hostility towards his greatest foes, as the evil one has against the human kind.

617. If we should examine with what eagerness he contends, here too would it be ridiculous to institute a comparison with men. If we should select the most fierce and cruel wild beasts, and wish to compare them with the madness of this, we should find that they were most gentle and tame in comparison: such fury does he breathe when he assails men's souls.

618. The time of conflict is in this world's battles brief, and in that short space there is many a truce; for the approach of night, weariness of slaying, time for food, and many other things are wont to give the warrior respite; so that he may put off his armour and take breath, and refresh himself with eating and drinking, and by many other means regain his former strength. But in our war with the evil one, there is no room for laying aside arms, nor can sleep be taken by him that would always abide unwounded. For one of two things must happen,—either to be disarmed and so to fall and perish, or to stand continually equipped and vigilant. He is ever standing with his array, on the watch for our relaxing, and he brings greater diligence to bear upon our destruction than we upon our own salvation.

619. The fact that he is not seen by us, and that his assault is sudden, (which in particular are the cause of innumerable mischiefs to those who do not always watch),[153] shows that this war is far more uncertain.

620. Would you then that I should command Christ's soldiers here? But this would be to be general for the devil; for when he who ought to marshal and array others, is the most unskilled and weak of all; such a one, betraying by his inexperience those entrusted to him, carries on war for the devil rather than for Christ.

621. But why do you groan? why weep? for my lot merits not lamentations now, but joy and gladness.

[BASIL.] But not mine, said he; but it deserves innumerable griefs. Even now I am scarcely conscious of the evils into which you have led me.

622. I came to you, anxious to learn how ever I should answer for you against your accusers; and you send me away after substituting another care for that I had. I no longer feel concerned how I shall answer them for you, but how I shall answer to God for myself and my faults.

623. I therefore pray and implore you, if you have any concern for my interests, 'if there be any consolation in Christ, if any comfort of love, if any bowels and mercies,'[154] —for you know that you more than all led me into this danger,—stretch out your hand, and by saying and doing what can restore me, do not bear to abandon me for the briefest space, but now more than before let us live together!

[CHRYSOSTOM.] 624. I answered smiling, How can I assist and be of use under

---

153 According to a different pointing the parenthesis ends at 'mischiefs,' and the sentence goes on,—'shows that this war is far more uncertain to those who do not always watch!'

154 Phil. ii. 1.

so great a burden of affairs? But since this is your pleasure, take heart, dear soul, for whenever you can find breathing time amid your cares, I will be with you, and will encourage you, and nothing shall be wanting that is in my power.

Hereupon, weeping yet more, he arose; and when I had embraced him and kissed his head, I led him forth, exhorting him to bear nobly what had occurred.

I believe, said I, that through Christ who has called you, and appointed you over His own sheep, that you will gain such boldness by this ministry, as to receive me also into your eternal tabernacle if I am in danger at that day.

www.ingramcontent.com/pod-product-compliance
Lightning Source LLC
Chambersburg PA
CBHW012208090526
44583CB00023BA/2991